MW01268032

"DATE!" is a Four-Letter Word, and Why You Should Never Use it

Rants, ramblings and reminders for the single man, in a time of digital dystopia.

By

Steven Provenzano

<u>Advance Praise for:</u>

"DATE!" is a Four-Letter Word,
and Why You Should Never Use It

"Great insights into male and female relationships that can help men avoid insecurity, dishonesty, fear, anger, and settling for the wrong relationship. Well worth it."
- Steve Yeschek, LCSW, CAMS-IV

"Essential for today's single man. Contains a wealth of useful insights, observations and information that all men, and the women they seek, would do well to consider."
- David Saunders, M.A

"A must-read. You and all women will be better off."
- J. Burns, M.M.

"A great read for guys who think they don't need help. Useful for women who want to get into the heads of guys."
- Jean R., Pharm. D.

"Are you kidding?"
"You need this book. Steven really knows this stuff."
- Steven's Mother from Liverpool, UK

"DATE!" is a Four-Letter Word,
and Why You Should Never Use it

U.S. COPYRIGHT: © 2018
Registered at www.Copyright.gov

By Steven Provenzano, President:
ECS: Executive Career Services & DeskTop Publishing,
Inc. An Illinois Corporation https://Execareers.com

Thanks to Assistant Editors Linda P., Scott H., Kristina G.,
Jean R., Tina D. , Carmein N., Dave S., and Steve Y.

PRINT / P.O.D. BOOK ISBN:
978-0-9633558-7-4

EBOOK ISBN:
978-0-9633558-3-6

Film rights available, contact the Author.

About the Author

Steven Provenzano is a Life Coach, Certified Professional Resume Writer (CPRW), Certified Employment Interview Professional (CEIP), former Corporate Recruiter, Improvisational Actor and author of ten books on expert resume writing, career marketing, and a GI Bride's immigration to America; more than 100,000 copies sold worldwide. His most recent career book is Top Secret Resumes & Cover Letters, 3rd Ed. the Complete Career Guide for All Job Seekers.

He is President of ECS: Executive Career Services & DTP, Inc. He and his staff have written thousands of resumes and Linkedin profiles for Fortune 500 clients worldwide.

He has appeared on CNBC, CNN, WGN, ABC/NBC in Chicago, on numerous radio programs, and in newspapers such as *The Chicago Tribune, The Wall Street Journal* and *Crain's,* and holds a BA in Journalism from Northern Illinois University.

His work is endorsed by Chicago Tribune Career Columnist Lindsey Novak, and top executives at firms such as Motorola, Coca-Cola and First Data Corp. For a free resume analysis, send your resume materials to: Careers1@Execareers.com; Site: https://Execareers.com.

Check our upcoming blog:
www.Dateisafourletterword.com

CONTENTS

Part One

NUTS
JERKS
Sex
The Disconnect
Fear and Emotion
Fish Love
Intention
Got Guts?
Rotten
Dodging Bullets
Commitment
Wisdom
The Chemistry of: CHEMISTRY
Science Proves How Sex Rewires the Brain
Conquest?
The Real Thing

Part Two

Damn Logic, Really
Stop Making Sense
Gut Check

Part Three

Get Honest with Yourself
Sincerity
Get Up, Stand Up
A Real Man

Part Five

Love is:
Your Standards
Takers and Givers
Over? Don't Block Yourself
You Can't Be Friends
There are No Good Breakups
Cut Your Losses
Get Out

Motivation, reminders and rants:

APPENDIX I – Easy
PANCREAS II – Alone Yet?
LIVER III – Faith, and Things to Remember

Notes to Yourself

<u>Bonus for print version:</u>

**Rock Stars Arrested
After Historic Flight**

Preface

This book is about right NOW, which is all you ever have.
It is about everyday life, and how you're living it: with grit,
determination, friends, community and humor... or without.
Time is running out, and you're not getting any younger.

Real men find the guts to face hard truths about themselves
so they can change and grow, without leaning on drugs,
alcohol, pornography, or anything else that only makes
things worse. Real men face and resolve their issues, a.k.a.
problems, head on.

If you're looking for fast sex, a quick "date" or a book on how
to conquer a pretty woman for another pointless roll in bed,
throw this book in the trash, or recycle. Do something good
for the environment; maybe someone else will find it and use
it.

Or would you like to "marry yourself"? Yes, that is actually
happening. It's a fallen world, but your task in life is to rise
above this world, and create a better life for yourself and
everyone around you. This book will help you do that; it is a
collection of personal experiences, insights, observations and
examples.

Leverage the tips in the first three parts of this book to get
clear and centered before even trying to connect with a
woman. Then try the fourth part. Stick with this book. If you
don't read it to the end, you won't get the big picture.

If you can't handle reality and raw truth in this digital
dystopia of fake, pretentious, shallow political correctness,
stop now.

PART ONE

NUTS

I was talking to a friend of mine about a girlfriend – she was all over the place – mentally that is.

"She's nuts!" he said. "They're all nuts!"

Now, of course not all women are nuts. He was talking about *emotional intelligence,* and when it comes to men, most women, about 92% according to my latest, non-scientific survey, do this:

They Follow Their Hearts.

Expecting a woman not to follow her heart, and make logical sense about whom she loves, follows, or accepts into her life, is like expecting a fish to jump out of water and go for a hike.

That's it. That's all you need to know. Now you can stop reading.

Actually, you need to know more, really, and it's not all about women anyway, it's about you:

Your insides, your motives, your drives, your fears and what comes out of your mouth.

It's about YOUR Heart.

Sound stupid?

Don't be a jerk.

<u>JERKS</u>

If women are nuts, men are jerks. We follow our eyes, our lust. Apparently, there's enough women who fall for this – or give us the benefit of the doubt – that more than 50% of marriages end in divorce.

Why do you want a woman? What do you want from her, and what can you give her (besides sex)? And if they're nuts (of course they're not *really* nuts) what does that make you for wanting them?

All too often, we act stupid and uptight around beautiful women. Why? We chase tasty junk food connections over Love and personal connection – then wonder why we end up alone, wanting, in a place of need.

That is not where a "Real Man" should end up.

Uncommitted and fearful, this is reality for too many men. "There's too many lone wolves out there," a Counselor and Life Coach once said, and he's right. What we think we want or need, is often wrong for us.

Maybe you never married. Or maybe you did, and it ended in a nasty, hateful, expensive divorce. I've seen too many friends and family go through this, and it's not necessary.

They should have known in their twenties to:

Stop. Wait. Hold Back. Grow up first. Get to know yourself better. Travel; see the world. Sow your oats now, and get it out of your system if you must. (Still chasing sex, alcohol or drugs? Don't get lost in that aimless, lonely world).

Then settle down – but don't settle – don't rush into anything.

Picture yourself 5-20 years down the road married to the woman you're with now, or the sexy ones at the bar, on the street, at the 7-11. Could you grow with her, through all the pain and confusion, the doubt, the rigors of a total, lifelong commitment?

If not, if you don't think you're ready to commit, do us all a favor:

Stay single, because:

"Whatever you give a woman, she will make greater. If you give her sperm, she'll give you a baby.. If you give her a house, she'll give you a home. If you give her groceries, she'll give you a meal. If you give her a smile, she'll give you her heart. She multiplies and enlarges what is given to her. So, if you give her any crap, be ready to receive a ton of shit!"
- Erick S. Gray

Sex

In this lightening-fast, A.D.H.D. culture, finding someone on Tinder to sleep with is common practice. Finding someone to wake up with... that's another story. Even if you're married to the most beautiful, sexy woman on earth, and spend 1-2 hours a night having sex; what about the other 22 hours?

Dozens of TV shows and thousands of websites center around sex and "hooking up". Yet as the fictional characters succeed in playing out their lust, we never see the aftermath. We don't see the emotional, physical and yes, chemical attachment following virtually all sexual encounters.

Where's the broken-hearted woman and the remorseful man, who can't explain his underlying concern for her?

Because that's how it goes in real life. And if you think quick sexual encounters make you a man, you're kidding yourself. Real men don't allow their loins (nor a woman's sex drive) to run their lives. They don't allow the lure of quick sex decide who to spend their free time with, talk to, open up to, share dinner with - or their inner-most secrets.

> *"Everybody's talking, and no one says a word.*
> *Everybody's making love, and no one really cares..."*
> - John Lennon, *Nobody Told Me*

The only men I've known who can survive hit-and-run sexual encounters seem to have little or no self respect for their bodies, their time, their energy, the women they meet, and least of all, their hearts.

In fact, many appear to have no heart whatsoever. How can any man have sex with a woman, even once, and feel no emotion or concern for that woman the next day? Can he really be that cold and sex-driven, selfish and all about the body? Brings to mind those empty-eyed, vacuous male models in Calvin Klein or Egoiste cologne adverts. Now there's a dark, lonely, selfish lifestyle; sign me up! **Never.**

The Disconnect

The internet, cell phones and computers are everywhere. We're more connected to – the internet – and less connected than ever to each other. Some of us would rather talk to our Amazon Echo than another person. Millions would rather text than talk, even for 2-3 minutes.

On *The Late Show with Stephen Colbert* the author of *Thank You for Being Late* and three-time Pulitzer Prize winner, Thomas L. Friedman recalled a conversation he had with U.S. Surgeon General Vivek H. Murthy, MD, MBA. He asked the doctor: "What's the most prevalent disease in America? Cancer? Diabetes? Heart Disease?"

He responded that it's none of the above. What's ailing us the most he said, was Isolation – a sense of being disconnected.

Look no further than the latest "dating" apps and social media for high-quantity, low-quality, shallow introductions, with little or no real connection: Tinder, Facebook, Pinterest, Match.com, eHarmony, OkCupid, Zoosk, Coffee Meets Bagel, OurTime, or Plenty of Fish for Christians. We're analog men stuck in a cold, disjointed, digital world, looking for Ms. Swipe-Right.

Single men – and women – are becoming self-contained, too comfortable in their isolation. We watch TV or movies, surf the net, find any distraction to take the place of a true companion, and the days roll on.

Fear and Emotion

For two decades, I've owned and managed a successful career services firm. Every day I talk to people terrified about moving forward, getting a decent job more quickly, or investing a few hundred bucks with an expert to help them shorten their job search.

Many of these people are top executives in the Fortune 500; they make six, even seven figures each year, and our services are a tiny percentage of their income.

These people *know* they can't do it all by themselves. Many of them sign up with us and are better for it. Still others reach out for our help and advice, use none of it, and go on their way, in total ignorance of the value of such a small investment.

Why is that? Is it our country, our prideful, stubborn, selfish culture, our upbringing or religious training? Perhaps all of the above; who knows.

The important thing to know is that fear and raw emotion are the two most powerful drivers behind whom we get involved with throughout our short lives. Think of it. Most "relationships" begin with a glance, a voice, a chance encounter. We spend far more time trying to decide which car or house to buy than we do deciding whom to trust, talk to, share deep secrets with, give our bodies to, give our hearts to, marry, (try to) spend the rest of our lives with, have babies with, or divorce.

Fish Love

Check out a video titled *Fish Love* by Rabbi Twerski on YouTube. In 2:03 minutes, the scholar gives excellent examples of what love is, and what it is not. Here's a quick outline:

"In our culture, the word *love* has almost lost its meaning. There's a story about a man enjoying a fish dinner. Another man sees his delight and asks: 'Young man, why are you eating that fish?' With great relish, the man replies 'because I love fish!' The other man says: 'Oh, well if you love the fish so much, why did you take it from the water, kill it and boil it? Don't tell me you love the fish, you love yourself. Because the fish tastes good to you, you took it from the water and killed it.' That man doesn't really love fish. He loves the way the fish makes him feel. He is really loving himself.

"So much of what we call love is 'fish love'. Let's say a young couple falls in love; what does that mean? That means the man saw in the woman someone whom he felt could provide for all his physical and emotional needs – and she saw the same in the man. And so it is with the love in our marriages and families.

We declare that we 'love' our spouses and our children, but the other person becomes a vehicle for our own gratification. Too much of what is called love is fish love. External love is not about what I'll get for myself, but what I can give to another. We make a serious mistake in thinking that we give love to those whom we love – in truth, we love those to whom we give. Self-love is a given; everybody loves themselves! True love is a love of giving, not of receiving."

Intention

So there you are on the couch with a new woman. Have you ever asked yourself:

Now what?
Is it really all about sex?

And whether you have sex or not, will you both end up arguing, cutting off the phone and moving on, never to speak again?

Play the tape forward – where do you see each other, together, in the next six months – in the next 20 years?

If your personal definitions of God include some sense of honesty, soul, love (even with a small l), peace, dignity, integrity, humility or grace, and of course commitment, then right at that moment, right there on the couch, ask yourself:

Why are you doing this? Where are you taking this?
Is it going somewhere - is there a future? Can you imagine yourself with this person - forever?

If not, then look deep inside, be honest, and ask yourself this:

Why bother?

End it then and there, no matter how "sexy" it feels, no matter how much dopamine is racing through your brain. Find the integrity to walk away. Don't be a dopamine dope.

Don't waste their time or yours.

Now that's guts.

Got Guts?

What gets me is when people stand around waiting for someone to "love" them, understand them and meet all their needs. That's impossible. No one can read your mind, and even if they could, why would they want to give their time, their life to you? What's in it for them? People like this need to get off their pedestal, get out, and love others – friends, strangers, family, and friends of friends, and expect nothing in return. That's how you get noticed by someone with potential.

You can only feel the love you have for another – you can't feel what another person feels. You may have mutual chemistry, and see signs of their devotion and sacrifice to you, but you cannot live in their head. From that viewpoint, just like the fish story above, it is better to love than be loved. That's because *you* can know and feel the elation, the satisfaction and fulfillment – and bring a woman to that same place.

What ever happened to true love and romance – when it all just came together, and pride, ego and selfishness were secondary? (Rent the Oscar-winning film *La La Land* for an example of this. There's still pride and ego, but Gosling and Stone connect with mutual respect; you can ignore the dancing .

We got lost in a world of fragmented text messages, emails, Facebook posts, tweets and "...leave your message at the tone...when you are finished, you may hang up, or press 1 for..."

What a joke.

There's still nothing you can buy or download to replace real conversation, preferably face to face, or on the phone if needed. Easier said than done. Now it's all about Match.com, eHarmony (he's harming me?) and the rest of that hide-behind-your-computer crap.

Every day we make personal choices to expand our unselfish love and direct it, to give it away for something meaningful and long-term, or let it die on a bed with a stranger.

If you believe there's no heart left in you, or anything like it, even if it's all about sex for you, no matter how old you are, or your last wife or girlfriend beat the crap out of you – inside and out – and even if it sounds weak or dumb or childish or non-macho, consider this:

In the end, it's about genuine emotion, sincerity, and love. Your physical needs – your bodily functions – remain in second place, like it or not. In fact, research has shown many men fall in love faster than women, and will express it earlier in a relationship.

I still believe all of us are born with some sort of love inside. It can still be there, it can still happen. It all starts with you: you need to believe that simple chemistry and attraction between a man and a woman is still possible.

Then, build on that, because:

If you let Love itself die – what, then, are you living for?

Even more mindless, heartless sex? More money?

Rotten

You hear it on TV, the radio, among your own friends: "Men are rotten, awful jerks...they only want one thing..."

Most of the time, it's from recently jilted women, and some of the time, it's true. I've also heard this from a respected Talk Radio Host. He typically makes sense – but attacks men regarding romance, marriage and attachment.

It's not that simple. Women can be just as lost, confused and impossible as men, and they need love too, of course.

But even if all men are idiots, (we're not, actually), the woman is still responsible for which idiot she allows into her life.

"Be more concerned with your character than your reputation, because your character is what you really are, while your reputation is merely what others think you are."
- Erick S. Gray

Dodging Bullets

Maybe you're like me: you could have been married several times by now, but you just weren't ready. You liked your freedom. Maybe you finally did get married, but like half of all marriages, it ended in divorce.

When people bug me about not getting married, I tell them anyone can get married – I want to stay married. I'm not avoiding marriage, I'm avoiding divorce, and marriage is the #1 cause of divorce. I want something that lasts.

Only my parents made it: Married when my Mother was 17, and Dad was 21, they stayed together 71 years, until sadly, Dad passed away in 2017. Family was everything to them: children, grandchildren or pals, the ones they had left. What a great, and rare example. They kept each other alive. I asked them how they did it, and what's the best thing parents can do for their kids; my Mother said, "It's simple, put the other person ahead of you, and cooperate. Love each other – in front of your children – make sure they see that every day."

As far as my sister and brothers and I could see, they did that, and they sacrificed their lives for us. My parents came home to each other and wanted to be there, to raise their children. Over the years, I saw that coming home to someone you actually like beats the crap out of being with a woman you hardly know. Back in their time it was all about:

Commitment

True commitment is:

- ➤ Self-sacrifice
- ➤ Putting the other person ahead of you
- ➤ Family (even if you never have children: supporting your parents, siblings and extended family)

Can you commit now? Are you ready?

First: A man must be totally sick of the "dating" game; he must be totally sick of being single.

THEN and only then, can/should he commit to a woman for the rest of his life. All else will most likely end in divorce - and nobody wants that.

I'll get into some practical steps you can take to avoid senseless dating (i.e.: repeated, shallow, awkward time spent with women you're not yet emotionally – or even physically – attracted to, yes, women do this too), and instead meet, emotionally connect with, and keep a decent woman you actually want to be with; but first this:

Wisdom

One of my favorite authors and speakers is 20-year veteran pastor, psychologist, M.Div. and Ph.D. John Ortberg. His books are everywhere, and one of them is *"Everybody's Normal Till You Get to Know Them."*

I've heard dozens of his lectures on all kinds of subjects. As a Counselor, he's heard it all, from drug, alcohol and sex addicts, to sadistic, abusive singles or married couples. Through humor, stacks of statistics and common (now exceedingly less common) sense, John helps people lost in their home-made maze of fear, loneliness and desperation.

He works with people looking for something, anything, to get past their addictions, or their co-dependency on others who are as lost as they are.

Leveraging Q&A, examples and careful listening, John helps guide those looking for some kind of dignity, joy, peace and that downgraded term no one feels strong enough to use anymore: *happiness*, which at the release of this book has now been fully replaced in the media and our colloquial with *excited*.

John gave an excellent talk about sex a few years back and for me, it all came down to this:

> **"You think you can separate your heart
> from your body – but you can't."**

It always starts simple, fun, playful. Then when it ends, no matter who ends it, it still hurts. A part of you gets nailed – and not in a good way. A piece of your heart, or soul, or whatever term you use for it, gets broken. That person takes a part of you with them – like it or not – believe it or not; and it takes time to get your head together, to refocus.

If it didn't hurt to end your last encounter, sexual or not, then it wasn't real (unselfish, uplifting Love, or even genuine emotional attachment) to begin with.

Now, some men (and women) still believe the best way to

get over a woman is to "get under another one" right away. I disagree, at least in the short term. That's because you're not complete. Your ego and pride will make you think you are, but it's a lie. That's your body talking, your selfish needs, your insecurity, and it's not true.

I know guys who can "pick up" and connect with strange women very quickly. They have the looks, the words, the eye contact. Too many women fall for men like this, quickly and without thinking, because they're lonely, and/or desperate.

> *"Women need a reason to have sex, men just need a place..."*
> - Billy Crystal (and Seinfeld)

Remember: women follow their hearts in the moment, or they follow what their eyes, or their passions speak to them. They just *fall* – and it feels like "Love" to them.

But a few weeks or months, or even years later after the sometimes angry, always toxic breakup, they move on. They see their former man flirting with everything that walks, always trying to prove himself, and never committing to anything long-term.

And the man? When she's gone, he's at it again – out for the conquest, the novelty, the short-term kicks that always leave him right where he started:

Alone

I know because I've seen too many men do this. Unwittingly, in my 20s, I was usually the one who broke it off – the involvement. But I always felt like I needed to stop and take time off to heal my heart, soul, etc., before starting anything new. I needed time to get myself back, in one piece, before getting involved again.

It's not about changing yourself for each woman – to meet her expectations. It's about knowing how you're perceived by at least most women, then learning and growing within yourself to become more in tune with the essence of truth, dignity and love itself. That essence is often buried deep inside, under your own fear, insecurity, and negative messages you've heard throughout your life.

The Chemistry of:
CHEMISTRY

The biggest sex organ is - the brain. Ever notice how hard it is to connect with a new woman when you've just broken up? That's because you're still *Chemically Attached* to your last partner. Even guys who think they're tough "bad boys" (who usually go home alone at night) can fake it for a while. But in the early stages, they come across as awkward, off, incomplete – and women sense this. They see it a mile away, and they will run from you, as they should.

Here's an article that backs this up. Now, whether or not you believe in any sort of Love, God, evil, etc., there's some undeniably useful, scientifically proven points here:

Science Proves Premarital Sex Rewires the Brain
By
JEREMY WILES / CONQUERSERIES.COM

There's a reason why breaking up from a sexual relationship is much more emotionally painful and much harder to forget than one that didn't involve sex. There are several neurochemical processes that occur during sex, which are the glue to human bonding.

Sex is a powerful brain stimulant. When someone is involved sexually, it makes him or her want to repeat that act. Their brain produces lots of dopamine—a powerful chemical, which is compared to heroin on the brain. Dopamine is your internal pleasure/reward system. When dopamine is involved, it changes how we remember.

The other part is oxytocin, which is designed to mainly help us forget what is painful. Oxytocin is a hormone produced primarily in women's bodies. When a woman has a child and she is breastfeeding, she produces lots of oxytocin, which bonds her to her child. For this reason, mothers will die for their child, because they've become emotionally bonded due to the oxytocin that is released when they're skin-to-skin with their child.

The same phenomenon occurs when a woman is intimate with a man. Oxytocin is released, and this makes her bond to him emotionally. Have you wondered sometimes why a woman will stay with a man who's abusing her? We now know that it's because she bonded to him emotionally - because of the oxytocin released during sex.

Men produce vasopressin, which is also referred to as the

27

"monogamy hormone," and it has the same effect as oxytocin has on a woman. It bonds a man to a woman.

These "bonding" agents narrow our selection to one person. That is wonderful in a marriage relationship but really bad in a dating relationship because you lose your objectivity when you're searching for your potential lifemate.

Impaired Judgment

According to neuropsychologist Dr. Tim Jennings, "When you have premarital sex, your reward circuitry is bonded to them [that person] now, and it will be much deeper and hurtful [to leave them]. Oftentimes, in breakups of people who've been sexually active, they can't tolerate the sense of emptiness, so they rush into another relationship. The neuro circuits did not have time to reset, and so they're impaired in their ability to bond with the next person, and they may become sexually active with them. This is just a repetitive cycle, and there are real impairments in bonding going on."

Becoming Bonded with Porn

These same neurochemicals are present when viewing pornography. A man will become bonded with whatever he is engaged in during the moment these chemicals are released. When your relationship is being carried on with an image, you become bonded to whatever you're viewing.

Dr. Doug Weiss, a marriage counselor, advises men to have eye contact with their wives during sex because they become bonded with that person. By doing this, he explains that, over time, individuals will decrease the "neural pathway to pornography and sexually inappropriate thoughts and beliefs, and glue to healthy sexuality to [their] wife. When your brain thinks sex, it thinks, 'Where's my wife?' And that is a great way to fight this battle."

Discovering how our minds were designed to operate by a Creator reveals truth in the way we are to live.

For someone viewing porn, one of the functions of oxytocin is to separate the experience and the excitement from the intensity of the shame. According to neuropsychologist Dr. Jes Montgomery, "Usually by the time they turn the computer off, they are already sinking into a sense of failure and shame, and the function of oxytocin is to tell the brain, 'Wait a minute. You don't want to remember that. You want to hold on to this excitement and this amazing magic that you just experienced.'"

Knowing how these neurochemicals interact and change the brain help us understand why sex is meant to be kept within the boundaries of marriage. You see the overtones here about God's design for His pure temple [a.k.a. your body]. This is another reason why the devil attacks our sexuality so much—because in attacking human sexuality, it actually interferes with human bonding.

So, for those practicing sex outside of marriage, they are creating a bond with their partner, thus inhibiting their discernment of whether they should remain in that relationship. God wired and designed our brains for a specific purpose: to bond ourselves with the person we marry.

Jeremy Wiles *is the executive producer and director of the* Conquer *series. Visit* <u>www.conquerseries.com</u>.

Thanks to Jeremy Wiles for this excellent article. This one hit home for me. I've seen a dozen well-meaning couples, some who call themselves Christian and some who don't, swear they will put off sex until they're engaged or married. Yet after a few months, all that intention disappears. Is that a good or bad thing? That's for you to decide.

However, by nature, when a man is sexually satisfied, he has very little reason to get married. Why surrender his freedom and independence? I've seen couples drag on for years like this. They seem contented and in love but most of the time, they wake up alone, and they still live alone, or live together but remain uncommitted.

Yes, we all like sex, it's amazing, fantastic. Can you enjoy sex to the maximum, without letting it dominate your life; without letting it decide whom you end up with, or making it your God?

Conquest?

You can pay for sex, lie for it, prowl the bar scene and get someone drunk for it. Just about anyone can get "married" to just about anyone else. Remember that divorce rate?

When he was ready to propose to his girlfriend, a buddy of mine said: "It's Time". He meant it was time to pick one... to start life over with a partner, the Real Thing. Time to put away childish things. He was 22 years old.

They got divorced anyway. They were too young and inexperienced. Life had become much faster, more hectic and self-centered than in my parent's day.

As a single man who's avoided marriage more than once, I'm glad I backed out: I wasn't ready, and I knew it. I could see we'd drift apart in the first few years and separate.

Marriage is easy to come by. Love, romance, devotion and long-term joy and peace with another person in your life, day after day, using the bathroom, the kitchen, the TV remote? That's something else.

Perhaps marriage is nothing more than placing your faith and trust in a process: an ongoing, daily process of placing your faith and trust in another person. You take the risk of placing their needs ahead of your own, and trust they will do the same for you; repeat until death.

For men of all ages afraid to "settle down" (yes, I hate that phrase too...it should be *rise up*), you are hereby notified that it's time for you to find a Life Partner. Not a maid or slave or a servant or sex object, or a "girl."

Even if you've been married before, stop running from - and start running to - your future. Find your destiny with a new partner, a genuine, grown-up woman, a woman who's at least remotely compatible to you in terms of intellect, likes/dislikes, values, physical stamina, and emotional honesty.

Impossible? Only if you think it is.

Just look around you. There are great, good looking women everywhere. OK, so most of them are already involved or married, but there's always a few out there, in between "boyfriends" (amazing we still use that word, well into our 40s and 50s).

And yes, looks really do matter, and don't let anyone tell you otherwise. From advertising to Survivor to The Bachelor, America is a looks-oriented culture. Most men desire a woman that's exciting to look at, to touch, to hold, to squeeze; and she doesn't have to be "perfect" either.

A friend who once said heaven might be an eternal orgasm also said:

"Nothing fills a man's senses like a woman."

He's right of course. How she looks, smells, feels, the touch of her skin, the sound of her voice, is intoxicating; I've been drunk on a few tall, cool ones myself. And when it's done, there's always the hangover...

But do you really want - or need - a "Trophy Wife?" Why? Exactly whom are you trying to impress?

The Real Thing

Lust and love have always been at odds. You need to get past sex because you're missing out, you're living beneath your privilege. There's just one other thing that's better for you, healthier and more fulfilling, and that's real love, with a woman you actually like, and who likes herself.

Of course, that's a rare thing to find in a world that's fast and cold and all about and sex. Take a long, hard look at yourself and ask: are you a victim of that very cliché? It is the hardest challenge for any man to rise above that world, to find his heart, hold it true, and wait for the real thing. It can be a long, lonely trip.

You can't make someone Love you. You can only call them, text them, pester them and stalk them until they file a restraining order. Yes, I am kidding. Don't ever do this.

"Love never fails..."

That's a quote from 1 Corinthians, that Bible verse you hear all the time at weddings (full quote is in the Appendix, below). Sound stupid? Even after a divorce, a hard breakup, the loss of a parent or a sibling, was "Love" fully lost, and can you prove it? Was it in the eyes of friends, family, the voice of the checkout girl? Was it not always there – and did you not see?

Just because sex or touching isn't involved, is there not "Love" of some type left in this sick world? Start there.

We have all heard: "Life is what you make it..." But it's also about what you do - or don't - allow to take place. It's about your interactions with EVERYONE.

What's the attitude you bring when you walk in the door – anywhere? How often do you take a superior, conceited stance to strangers? That's exactly how I am when I don't get enough sleep – with the checkout girl, the front-desk guy, the bank teller.

What are you doing (or not doing) to allow yourself to *feel?*

Pry your eyes open, and find some kind of connection with others again because:

All else is pointless

None of this is easy, of course. Hey, if falling and staying in Love with a great woman was easy, we'd all be there already.

All of the good, kind, humble men would have great wives, and all the bad-boy rats would be out on the streets, justifiably alone. There'd be no crime, no pain, and no need for me to write this book. Such is the world.

However, if you read the rest of this book (I heard about half of all books purchased in the U.S. are never completed), you'll find ideas to get off the endless "dating" cycle, build a place in your heart for just one more person, *align* yourself with real Love, and attract a decent woman you can build a life with.

That beats the hell out of chasing the d-word in bars, online, or anywhere else.

PART TWO

Damn Logic, Really

If a woman has to *think* about being with you,
she doesn't want to be with you. Period.

"Thinking, logic, analysis," etc., only does one thing:

it destroys love.

The very greatness of love is that it is **Not Logical.** Of course love isn't logical and doesn't make sense; that's why we want it, it's a better reality.

We strive for love precisely because it is a beautiful, warm passionate escape from logic and reason itself.

At best, it's a short, or long-term vacation from being
wrapped up in ourselves.

Logic is the enemy of Love.
Remember the Talking Heads?

Stop Making Sense

Why? Because logic and making sense is boring – it is not what brings lovers together. What brings them together is attraction, chemistry, that unspeakable warm and honest place you find in their eyes – and they must see in yours – usually, but not always - at first sight.

Sound silly? Ask any Spanish Bullfighter or Flamenco dancer. They may look scrawny and wimpy in those black tights, but they're being chased by more women than you. Guaranteed.

Love is where logic ends, and the heart begins. As hard to describe as a beam of light: particle or wave? How you perceive it depends on where you stand right here and now, the pair of eyes you use to seek it; what you believe in and stand for.

You show that to others by your actions, deeds and words; by what you seek (or bring to) everyday encounters with – everyone; how you find "fulfillment" in your life; what matters most to you.

Just as ancient religions avoided speaking the word God, there's no need (or possibility) to describe or label Love itself. Talk is still cheap, and always secondary to emotion and chemistry.

You'll know when you're in it; there's a difference between loving and being *in Love*. For example: I love my mother, but I'm not *in Love* with her.

If you think you've given up on connecting with a woman, maybe that's good: now your selfish ego, pride and lust are gone, or at least in second place, the first step to creating fertile ground for new possibilities.

True connection is far bigger and better than your own ego, sex drive, etc. In fact, sex may be the farthest thing from your mind – when you first meet a woman that makes you forget everyone else.

You will only see that when you're clear, open and honest with who and what you are. When you accept your flaws and fully believe in your heart, or Love, or God – and stand in your own place of **humble peace.**

I must be clear: this is not feminine or weak, or meek, or un-masculine, or stupid: **It is essential to your health and your future.**

Numerous studies have shown that lonely people are less healthy, and generally live shorter lives than those with strong, loving connections to friends, family, community and their wives/husbands. How long do you want to live?

Gut Check

Ask yourself: is your heart still intact? Are you uncomfortable just reading that question? Does it seem like a dumb, childish, pansy-ass question...or are you just afraid of giving it a dignified answer?

You probably still have a heart; just reading this book is a good sign. It's in there somewhere. Hey, if I can even mention the word in the first few pages of this book, the least you can do is admit you have one, and not let yourself feel weak or stupid for doing it.

You gotta touch her heart, quickly, and you can't do that without expanding and showing YOUR heart, your integrity, your security and decency, as often as possible.

And while there is no such thing as certainty when two people meet, women at least need the illusion of certainty.

In his book *Blink: The Power of Thinking Without Thinking,* Malcolm Gladwell claims that we make up our minds about each other in just a few seconds after first meeting, and I agree.

Numerous studies point to the fact that both men and women - especially women when it comes to romance, quickly "decide" if they:

> Want to talk to you.
> Believe what you're saying.
> Want to continue talking with you.
> Think you're a total jerk and race for the door.

While there are rare exceptions (when a woman gets past the visual and actually talks/listens to the guy for few minutes), this is also when they "decide" if they want to marry you, have your babies, and move to that little cabin in the Rockies, on a river bend in Southern Colorado.

Your heart must be there from the start. Whether you call it being aligned with God, The Universe, Beauty, Your Core, Your Essence; you simply must show up, always, no excuses, 100%. You don't have a soul, you *are* a soul, like it or not.

This is essential at first contact: not logic or perfection, but at least the *illusion of perfection.* You must show up, all the time, fully and completely.

"in the beginning was the myth, chapter one starts like this: blank and calm and full of expectancy. I'm standing exactly where I'm supposed to be."
- Poi Dog Pondering

For more detail on this, check out a new book: *Present over Perfect: Leaving Behind Frantic for a Simpler, More Soulful Way of Living,* by Shauna Niequist.

Ultimately, anything you conjure up to say in the moment doesn't really matter to her...it's the feeling that matters, the vibe, that's all she's following. She's looking for your core, your truth, your essence, the substance; she's looking for a sign of God/Love in your eyes.

A man we've all heard of put it like this:

"Remembering that you are going to die is the best way I know to avoid the trap of thinking you have something to lose. You are already naked. There is no reason not to follow your heart."
- Steve Jobs

PART THREE

Get Honest with Yourself

It's not hard to understand your strengths and positive qualities. We all want to believe we're OK, great, even excellent compared to those around us.

That's because when we live totally by our own standards: *we all think we're OK and righteous.* Who doesn't want to believe that about themselves?

If you think you're tough, are you tough enough to face your greatest weaknesses? Your arrogance, ignorance, hubris or lack of forgiveness? Could these traits (often subconscious) have played a role in destroying old connections, with women or other men - your brothers?

You can't fake Sincerity, that's why it's called:

Sincerity

There is no generic method to attract women, because they are all unique. Your look, voice and mannerisms may attract one woman, and repulse another. The best you can do is find – and sincerely respect and appreciate – a woman for who she is – right where she is.

If you're out chasing women, or morphing/changing yourself into what you think women want, you have already failed, and yet, this is incredibly common.

Even worse, you have failed yourself.

To some degree, we can all sense true sincerity, honesty, dignity, integrity – and the lack of it. This is especially true of

43

women seeking to connect with an honest, genuine, humble, yet solid man with backbone.

> *"Be yourself, everyone else is taken."*
> - Oscar Wilde

I always liked *English Man in New York,* by Sting. He reminds us to be ourselves - regardless of what anyone says.

Whether you know it or not, most women can see the real you, behind the show. They can tell if you're all there – 100% free of any other attachments – to your last girlfriend, ex-wife, whomever.

That's why you must be free and clear after each attachment. Take the time to be centered in solitude – to get back to the best, genuine, clear-minded YOU you can possibly be.

You must take time off to break that chemical connection. It may take weeks or months; it doesn't matter how long, just do it. Because even if you do fake it and gain her interest, it will eventually fall apart.

Don't "act" like a man; be one.

But there's that paradox. Becoming a better man means <u>letting go</u> of your selfish ego, pride and lust, and letting true Love, God, emotion, or your best term for it, take over. Whether you call it Magic, Chemistry, Love, Fate, or God's will, understand this: it is not of your own making. It is not about you: your ego, your pride, your lust or selfishness. Trouble with that? Keep reading.

Here's a short article from Drs. Judith and Bob Wright. I attended one of their programs a few years back. Check out their numerous books related to self-motivation and greater satisfaction. The article   begins with a quote:

"One day, when we are no longer together on this earth, I want to know that you knew me."
- David Morris Schnarch

Ever been afraid to be yourself around others? To be **truly, genuinely you?** Maybe you're afraid to show your quick temper. Or that you're proud of your accomplishments and want to show them off. Or maybe you're afraid to show that you're afraid!

You're not alone. Many of us are afraid to be ourselves, thinking that we'll be rejected if we reveal certain aspects of ourselves.

But **to experience true intimacy, you need to be fully yourself.** You need to share more of you. According to researcher David Schnarch, intimacy is the process of confronting who you are and sharing yourself with your partner, otherwise known as **self-validated intimacy.**

When you are more real, more authentic, more yourself, you will **attract more people** and be able to have deeper, more intimate relationships. And you'll have more opportunities to feel known.

This week, focus on being yourself 100 percent. Tell your boy/girlfriend what he/she means to you. Engage in a meaningful conversation with your coworkers at lunch. Share your ideas in the next board meeting.

Express yourself fully, be present - be YOU! **Be spontaneous. Be outrageous. Be stupendous. Be vulnerable.** Have fun!

All the best,

Dr. Judith Wright and Dr. Bob Wright

*Schnarch, David Morris. **Passionate Marriage**: **Love**, **Sex** and Intimacy in Emotionally Committed Relationships

Get Up, Stand Up

The Doctors Wright are – right. Unless you want to be running from one failed encounter to the next, you need to start working on these things now, today, using all possible methods:

- ➤ Stop – be still
- ➤ Vent your frustrations; take a Karate class and beat the crap out of something
- ➤ Pray and/or meditate on what the best *you* would look like, and how to get there – so it's natural, not fake
- ➤ Join a health club, at least for the Winter months
- ➤ Get "centered"
- ➤ Relax and rest; less Starbucks, more sleep
- ➤ Try basic Yoga, at least 1-2 times to get the idea, then at home when you can; no need to think of any religion during this
- ➤ Talk to a shrink – at least for a few hours
- ➤ Be genuine, all the time; expose your flaws to people you trust, so they may be overcome. Get honest feedback; find and leverage support. It's all around, but it starts with facing up to who and where you are in life - *right now*
- ➤ Travel outside the U.S. to experience different cultures, lifestyles, art, and how men and women in different countries interact and respond to each other
- ➤ Get back to you, yourself, in a state of mind you can live with. You're stuck inside yourself 24 hours a day; what else is more important?

Stand in confidence, but get rid of the selfish arrogance, the pride, the lust, the impatience, the ego, *if only to discover what's left.*

> *"Be independent of the good opinion of other people."*
> - Abraham H. Maslow

A Real Man

A real man is unafraid of what his pals - the guys - might think. He stands without fear of his heart, mind, soul, emotions and his own (usually temporary) isolation. That's where you find true connection to God, the Universe, Love, energy, etc. Inside of YOU is where true love and romance begins. It has always been there, just buried under stress, materialism and the nonsense of society, the media, or the daily stream of political insanity.

That's the place where a genuine, warm, romantic, sexy, true connection with a woman can happen. Yes, I know because: I've been there.

Now it's your turn.
Yes, life is short.
Are you strong enough to grow and change?
Don't blow it. Do it.

What do Women Want?

I heard a guy yell this at some boring seminar last year: "What do women want?" he called to the speaker. I should have grabbed him afterward and slapped him around. The short answer is:

A lack of negatives, and a true, strong, steady, reliable, predictable (but not boring) dignified heart.

When all is said and done: You've been there, done it, seen it, made your mistakes and lost out on great opportunities...you need to get back to your center.

49

Alright: back to your childish, little kid heart.

Without that, you got nothin' anyway. You're just another meat popsicle, a dweeb in nice shoes, a mongrel with a baseball hat at the bar after the game with your friends, gawking and cat calling to the pretty women two tables over (hey, be glad they're at least that far away, they'd stroll over and kick 'ya in the cojones).

When you get back to your soft, gooey center, you'll find it's still, well, gooey. But you're getting closer to what women want when you strip away all the false idols in film, TV and music; all the dumb pickup lines; all the nervous fronts we find ourselves in because we fear feeling rejected by someone who doesn't even know who the hell we are.

Get back to a time before your high school sweetheart or first lover told you it was OVER, Dammit, and don't come back, and "you'll never find anyone else…ever!"

Never use other men to make you look "better"

There's an ex-high school acquaintance who mentions me whenever there's an attractive woman around. He shows up at social events, even a local church, to hit on unsuspecting single women – strictly for sex. He even tells them "we went to school together" and "we were friends" when we weren't friends at all. Still, he feels the need to use me as his connection, a step up – some kind of reference to meet women I know as friends.

When I heard of this and spoke the truth about him to others, he turned. Now he talks me down and lies about me behind my back – to any woman he sees me talking to. He's courteous to me when we're both in front of others, of course.

I've heard women call him a sex predator. Fortunately, many of the women are on to this, and they warn each other.

We've all seen this – in real life, the movies, everywhere. It's incredibly annoying. People like this are actually weak, needy, possessive, childish and most of all, insecure.

Your response? Most of the time, blow it off, and make sure you don't do this yourself. Rise above it all and stay quiet. But if you hear of a specific instance of this type of person lying about you to others – call or confront him directly and demand that he stop, right now. I finally had to do this with *the predator.*

Stand up for yourself, and above the nonsense

Only weak, insecure men feel the need to use others as stepping stones to manipulate others to get sex, time, attention, or anything else in life.

Stand strong, calm, and clear in your own right and eventually, you will be noticed.

Reverse Psychology – On You

This all makes sense; but what if you're stuck? What if you've failed so many times, and you're ready to give up?

<u>Then Own It. Believe it.</u>

For one minute, believe the lie that you are indeed at the "end." That it will never get better – you will never meet a decent woman and find a good, committed connection.

Stare that in the face – and believe it – just for now.
Take a few minutes to think about that, really.

Now, doesn't that sound stupid? You're right, it is.

No matter how smart or cool you think you are, you cannot predict the future. I've been in that lost, lonely place many times - but I always came out of it. The trick is to use that time and place to rebuild and get back to the best, core self you can possibly be.

Think back; you've probably done this, without even knowing it. I failed many times, then finally saw the pattern. It took time, but I learned to practice this to clear my mind and stand on my own two feet with, if nothing else, a clear heart. Yes, I still fail, but I keep going, and most women appreciate this.

Feelings, and Emotional Intelligence

Even with true sincerity, no one can ever feel exactly what you feel. Still, a woman can relate and connect, deeply and emotionally. She can support, uplift and sustain you the best she can, driven by an illogical heart (to her it makes sense of course, but it's all based on pure emotion, at least in the beginning).

Yes, she can sense true attraction and sincerity in your eyes – even fall in love at first sight – but that's not the same as knowing your real, long-term intentions: fear or desire for commitment, eventual loyalty, faithfulness and need (or lack of need) for marriage. Only God (or your personal source/sense of genuine truth, peace, honesty and love) and you can know that.

Given this truth, it's amazing men and women get along at all. It all goes back to that core desire of men to have sex, and of women not to be alone and to have babies. The same friend who said women were nuts said, "If women were really smart, they wouldn't talk to us at all." He had a chip on his shoulder. He had been playing the anonymous dating game far too long.

I know plenty of intelligent women. Overall, if more women were in charge of cities, states and nations, there would be less war and famine, and overall, the world would be a better place.

> *"When God created man, she was practicing."*
> - Rita Mae Brown

Actually, I don't agree with this. God is not a he or a she

53

(unless you're referring to Jesus, of course), and God created us equal, but thankfully, very different. It would be a bland, boring life if we were all the same.

> *"If the world were perfect, it wouldn't be."*
> \- Yogi Berra

PART FOUR

The Real Man's Non-Rules to Non-Dating

Alright, enough of that sappy, emotional stuff for now. Why did you pick up this book?

Are you looking for:

1. A one-night stand (or a two-or-more night stand for some pointless, fleeting, meaningless sexual pleasure that leaves you just as empty the next day)? If sex is the foundation for being with a woman, it will almost always end badly, and you're back where you started.

2. A Girlfriend, however you define it?

3. A Relationship? (Yet another, heavy, dreary joy-killing word. The "R" word: to be avoided at all cost, just like the "D" word. When pressed in conversation with a woman, try using Relation-boat - adds humor. Just don't use Relation-dinghy, way too perverted).

4. A mother figure to marry you; to wash your clothes and dishes?

5. A solid, one-on-one, truly respectable, genuine partner, someone to laugh and share your life with; someone to witness your life while you witness hers? Someone who can keep up with you in deep conversations, deep love and deep troubles? A Woman - not a girl - to share your deepest feelings and fears? (And yes, you have them, admit it.)

6. Or is it really just about SEX again?

Why You Should Never Say "Date"

Never say *date,* because it slaps a label on the encounter:

> It is Logical
> It Defines
> It Boxes in
> It Controls
> It Destroys
> It Wrecks the Mystery
> It Spoils Chemistry

The best d-word substitutes:

Get together... hang out... meet for...go out sometime... (exactly where is a negotiation that needs to happen).

Get a drink...grab a "bite" (don't use the other d-word...dinner...way too heavy, at least in the beginning).

In a woman's heart, definitions like these kill the romance, the emotion, the spontaneity that might just happen on its own. You come off as predictable, and nobody wants that – even if they say they do.

Instead: let it be. Let it unfold. Act in confidence, be yourself, and go with the flow: the mutual energy, the warm feeling you get when you're with her. If you don't feel those things early on, walk away.

A woman I connected with once told me about a previous encounter. On their second meeting, the guy held up a glass for a toast and proclaimed: "To our new RELATIONSHIP!"

She dumped him immediately.

Why You Don't Want to "Date"

You think you want the d-word, but you don't. Here's why:

<u>Dates are for two people who don't know
if they like each other.</u>

If dating is so great, why do your friends and family complain about it all the time?

Now, you may call a one-time meeting with someone – through an online dating site a "date" if you want, but again, don't speak the word. Besides, those aren't *dates* in any sense of the word of course – they're just one-time meetings.

After that, you're either getting closer/involved/seeing each other, or you're not, and that's always up to what the woman wants/sees/perceives/needs – what she will allow.

The d-word amounts to spending (too often wasting) time with certain women even when you lack that rare, true, emotional connection. If a woman asks about the d-word, tell her you'd rather take time to know who she really is.

Every moment spent with a woman who's wrong for you, is a moment apart from the woman who could be right for you.

Alternatively, when I see a genuine couple: a man and woman walking hand-in-hand, relaxed and just enjoying time together, I don't think of the d-word – I see two people who are truly, warmly, *emotionally involved* or *seeing* each other, even *in love* with each other.

If that's what you really want - to meet a genuine, decent, grown up woman who's at least working on her issues as much as you are; if you want an emotional, passionate, eye-to-eye connection, a true, long-term situation (avoiding the "R" word again, relationship, but that's really what it is), then you're on the right track.

In the end, I'm not really anti-date, I'm pro-meeting as many new women as possible (again, only if you're now clear and centered), keeping smart emotional boundaries, and seeing what happens. That can be a good meeting of two unknown people open to anything. I am pro-connection, pro-chemistry, pro-romance, and pro-possibility of a future with someone who's right for you. Too often, what counts as "dating" is plastic, empty, a place for people who've lost their hearts, and are too hung up on themselves, their past, or their self-centered feelings of independence.

People like this would rather stare at their computers or phones, and sleep by themselves every night, than lift a finger to let themselves fall in love or truly connect with another human being. They are living in fear, which controls too many conversations, personal decisions, elections and lives.

Just ask her out

Take her out for food, water, ice cream, beer, wine, coffee, tea, a walk on the beach, a hike in the woods, anything, because it doesn't matter. (Studies have shown we communicate better when walking – our brains are more engaged.)

Whatever you choose, it's only a time and place to talk and know more about each other – to get more connected.

Align Yourself with True Connection

We all like checklists. Here's a damn checklist:

1. Keep your Dignity.

Stop "chasing" and trying to "impress" women. Just like a rabbit in the forest, they run when they see anything that looks hungry chasing them. Wouldn't you? Their emotional radar, their intuition, is usually very clear: they can tell when a man appears desperate, or just out for superficial physical contact – with no idea of genuine love or attachment. They can see it a mile away, even if you can't. Learn from this, and seek the opposite. Remember, the eyes are the window to the soul, and they'll see right behind yours. They'll see your true motivation, often before you do yourself.

2. Calm down, relax, loosen up, be yourself – again; don't get too heavy; you're not God, (thank God).

Maybe you're anxious, desperate, or just plain horny. Guess what? Get in line behind dozens of other guys just like you who've hit on them over the past two months. Because you know what? They don't care. They just don't care how much you want or 'need' them, or their bodies. Remember: on first meeting, all a woman really cares about of course is: *how you make them feel.* Right here and now. In the first few seconds you meet. Period. Saying or doing stupid, embarrassing things is like slouching, we don't realize we're doing it at the time, but people notice, and it hurts us romantically and socially. Break your old patterns. Walk the fine line of *speaking and doing* the creative, right thing as much as you can, without trying to control everything.

"And think not that you can direct the course of love; for love, if it finds you worthy, directs your course."
- Kahlil Gibran's *The Prophet*

3. Realize that because of #1 and #2, above:
It really, really doesn't matter what sort of car you drive, how big your house (or anything else) is, what clothes you wear (as long as they're not ripped and you don't smell), or how much money you have. How could a woman possibly know anything about your bank account, car, etc., when you first meet? Can you recall if that was even discussed when you first met any of your previous girlfriends? It was just you and her then, connecting to the present situation – and nothing else mattered.

If love were up to us, we'd all be screwed

If money and material things brought us true love and romance, then rich people would have all the love and joy in this world; but look at how many of them are lonely and miserable with all their *stuff.* Truth is, money and material things can only bring us sex, and sex without love is always a dead-end street.

"We make a living by what we get. We make a life by what we give."
- Winston Churchill

On a trip to Cairo, Egypt a few years ago, I saw some of the poorest, yet happiest kids I've ever seen, laughing and playing in the streets. Unless you're a grade-school teacher, how many children of wealthy – or even middle-class Americans have you seen laughing lately?

4. Stay positive, upbeat, strong and most of all: confident. I mean ALL the time – or as much as possible. You never know when, where or how you'll meet the next best woman you've never met. Be ready, be clear, be calm. Things change, sometimes overnight.

> *"Sometimes, you gotta act like you just don't care."*
> - DG, a friend

I can't recall how I met most of the women I've been involved with, or what I said. I didn't plan my words. It's usually by chance, but the ground was fertile: the right place, the right time; it all just happens. Remember the Boy Scout motto: "Be Prepared." Hey, if it works for kids in green shirts...

> *"Love is what happens to men and women who don't know each other."*
> - W. Somerset Maugham

5. Don't over-prepare; keep a sense of humor. Stop striving for "perfection", you'll never get there.

If you're in love with yourself, get over it

Women don't expect 100% perfection. What most women want is simply this: safety, a change, something new. They're tired of the same old pitches, problems, crass jokes, strange behavior and arrogance. Subtract all of this from your attitude asap, and you're already ahead of 99% of the single guys out there with the same old tired lines.

"Who ever loved that loved not at first sight?
It lies not in our power to love or hate,
For will in us is overruled by fate."
- Christopher Marlowe
(Used by Shakespeare in As You Like It.)

Get Somewhere with Her

Right from the start, two things must happen:

1. The man initiates and takes the lead.
2. The woman takes his hand (either physically or mentally/emotionally, as is more often the case) and she follows, immediately, *without doubting.* You'll most likely see this in her eyes, or not. You will both think about/consider your situation later of course, but by then, your attached.
3. All else is doomed.

Women: you must make yourself emotionally vulnerable to connect; don't be afraid to trust a man at the start. Give us a chance – then if we mess it up and you bail out, it's our fault.

Never take advantage

Connecting with a good woman is a privilege – not a right – honor that privilege. If you don't like or respect her much, be a gentleman and walk away. Leave her for someone else.

You may even let her think: *it was her idea to walk away.*

Now THAT'S a True, Dignified Man.

Wanting Contact

Asking a woman to call or email you is like asking a cute squirrel on the sidewalk to pick up a phone and dial a number. It's not gonna happen...and it shouldn't...it would only go against the laws of nature.

Calling and (warmly) pursuing her is <u>your job,</u> not hers. You may be a raging bull, but she's the gatekeeper.

Never get emotionally ahead of a woman – you will quickly lose her respect – and then her.

Mr. Entertainment

James Bond and Jim Carrey: You must be both, at least at first. Being taller may play a subliminal part, but that's not a deal breaker; pile up your hair if you have any; wear thicker shoes.

Once emotionally involved, however, you're still not "dating", you are:

Seeing each other
Hanging out
Liking each other, or even:
Attached

Drop the Pursuit

As mentioned: a woman shuts down and runs when she feels excessively pursued. You might be the best guy she's met in years, but she'll never know that if you push too hard.

Even worse, she quickly loses respect for you.

Who can blame her? If she's remotely good looking, she's being stared at, and hit on by sleazy guys all the time. *How can she not harbor resentment?*

Draw her into you by being a man who is genuinely:

Safe. Kind. Sincere. Generous. Warm. Fun. Romantic.

However, don't 'push' these attributes. Instead, become them, and they will be self-evident.

Watch your words, and body language

Research proves that up to 85% of communication in non-verbal. Whether through too much touching or flowers and gifts when you first meet, you will quickly destroy the mystery, and the tension required for genuine attraction and romance.

This is a fatal, and all-too common mistake among lonely, desperate men. They push too hard up front, they over-do it; they focus on material, outward things, rather than connecting with the woman herself: her heart, her feelings, her thoughts, her family, her life – what's really behind her eyes. Your flowers, your gifts mean nothing, if you don't first express warmth, safety and love to her through your body language and words.

Be the opposite of an anonymous date; be the exception.

Tension: Live in the Tension

In Rob Bell's book Sex God, (no, he doesn't mean you, or *that* either), he talks about living in the tension that happens between men and women when they're attracted, and he's right on. If you're looking for a soft, easy ride, or want to rush into bed, slam on the brakes. Because even if that succeeds, you've already failed; it won't last. In the end, you're another day older.

Live in the Tension. The Desire, the Need, the Expectation. Slowly build something better, and real, together.

Depending on the situation, it might be best to hold back as much as possible. Make no assumptions. If you really want her, then draw her out of her shell, where many women retreat from all the pushy, senseless men who've advertised one image and delivered another.

Men may have lied and wasted her time, body and emotions; wasted her heart, and wasted her essence. She doesn't need that, and neither do you.

Stand strong, cool down, be confident, and most important:

Slow Down

As a man, you must take the lead, but slow down to her pace. You can and must initiate contact, but never get ahead of her, physically or emotionally.

She sets the pace, and you tune into it. Like it or not.

She then grants you the illusion of "being in charge" and "taking the lead," when of course, it's up to her how much love or connection she allows in her life.

Remember: abuse this privilege, and you will lose her, quickly.

Be Different: Be Patient

If you really want to make a genuine, strong, loving connection with a kind, strong (but not selfish or bitchy) woman who values true love and commitment over fast sex, then you need to be very patient.

Dig deep inside the second you meet, and bring out something different, warm, spontaneous, positive, centered. Take risks. Give her some – any – unique reason to see you again. If she thinks you're anxious or going too fast, you'll look just like a typical lonely, desperate guy who's hitting on her, and she'll back away.

This is not a race, not a fake reality show, and there are no cameras on you. There's no one to impress; you don't have to tell your friends about the new woman so they'll think you're cool. Keep it private, and personal if you want something real – something that can last. I see men talk too much and mess this up all the time.

Keep it personal. Listen closely, talk less. Read her eyes, her body language, her tone of voice. Calm down and ride the wave – enjoy your time together.

67

Things happen, and go forward (or don't) in their own time, <u>not yours.</u>

You've heard it before, and it bears repeating:

Prove that you like/love yourself, and others tend to do the same.

Friends

It's hard to get close to a woman once you're in her friend box. That's because you're not "new" anymore. They know things about you, but only in a general, friendly sense. You may indeed be the best man in the world for her, in the long run. However, for a woman to let you out of her friend box to become something more, of course, would be to admit she was wrong about you in the first place – and of course, in her mind, *that's just not possible.*

You've heard it: You never get a second chance to make a first impression, and we all judge each other by that first impression, like it or not. If it's no fun to be around you, what's in it for them? They certainly don't need a pickup line. They need a human.

Are you a Christian? An Atheist? A Mormon, A Muslim?

In the long-term, these things matter, but at the start, who cares?
Not the woman, at least not when you first meet, hey, that would make sense. Just like you, they make sense at their jobs all day: BORING.

Avoid arguments at all cost...at least in the first few weeks. When you have your first real argument, and stay together: then you know you're attached...like it or not.

Besides, if you have an argument and come off as truly angry in her eyes, whether you have a valid point or not, you'll be dismissed as: Unsafe; Bad; Weird.

In the first few weeks, if you appear hurt in her eyes, you may be dismissed as: Weak, Odd, Childish, or worst of all: "Too Sensitive". There goes the respect: and then, of course, both of you are lost.

And what good is that?

Decipher the Code

If a woman calls you "Nice", she typically does NOT want to get emotionally involved.

If a woman says goodbye by shaking hands, or says "take care," she does NOT want to see you again.
(Unless she only wants to be friends, of course)

The same is true if you hug each other,
and she pats you on the back more than once.

If you see these signs early on, don't call, text or send an email. You can be pals, and maybe more if she reaches out, other than that, don't bother.

Combinations

You may be the best man – the right man – for a certain woman; but attracting the right one is like cracking a safe: they all have different combinations.

While this is true, you can't think of it that way - it's self-defeating, discouraging, and gets you nowhere. Get rid of that thinking, NOW. Besides: no one wants to hear your gripes and complaints; who cares?

See a shrink, a close friend, a pastor or a priest. Get on your knees and talk to God – read about Jesus and selfless love. Get it all out if you must: the pain, the frustration, the lack of closure. Because most of what passes for "communication" these days, is NOT. It's only a reason for single men and women to remain:

SINGLE

In these times, surrounded by billboards, email, social media, sexting and texting:

ONLY the POSITIVE prevails.

Ultimately, both sides, men and women, want to be in charge of when something starts – or doesn't. Only true, vulnerable hearts connect for anything meaningful. Stand Tall and Speak Up. Stop texting and speak in PERSON if possible, or on the PHONE if you must, but then face to face, and right between the eyes.

Fear is NON-EXISTENT, and only stands for:

F alse
E vidence
A ppearing
R eal

And no one sees it but you; therefore:

MAKE A CONSCIOUS-MAN'S CHOICE RIGHT NOW:
DECIDE TO STOP SEEING FEAR.

In American society at least:
nice guys often do finish last

71

"Nice guys" are too often seen as weak. Try to be aware of when you're giving this perception, valid or not, then adjust and move on. No one likes a pushover.

Other than a smile and eye contact, a woman does not pursue – she is pursued. She then either allows the encounter to move forward, or not.

This is not a slight at women at all: They make fantastic decisions. They also make great doctors, lawyers and politicians. They listen better, and often communicate with greater detail than most men. The women I hire at my company are typically better writers than men. Most women I meet have incredible wisdom and patience.

In fact, no matter what your intentions, and before any real involvement can happen, engrave this on your forehead:

She Needs to Think It's Her Idea – Even if It's Not

Whatever you say or do, for whatever reason, nothing goes forward until the woman feels right and takes action, or allows you to take action and move forward.

You getting her number and calling means nothing if she doesn't answer or call back. Ultimately, the ball's in her court, and she needs to feel it's worthwhile to talk to you. It's her decision (albeit based on her emotions: sensible, misguided or otherwise) to deal with you at all – to give you a chance.

Because women follow their hearts, their emotions, their initial gut feelings about you, a.k.a.: the first impression you make, they latch on to your tone of voice, and secondarily, the first words out of your mouth.

It doesn't matter if it's in a bar, a church, a forest, a junkyard or a mansion: if mutual connection and attraction doesn't happen quickly, then most of the time, you're toast.

In fact, burnt toast. You're outta here. Have a nice day. She's on to the next first encounter: the next chance to feel swept off her feet. Unfair? Absolutely. Note to women: we can sweep you off your feet – but that's much easier when you stick your feet out. You need to do better at this. Don't assume we're all the same, and only want one thing. Give us a sign, a smile, a look, a touch on the arm, anything. We can't read your mind, just your actions. When you're at ease, you put us at ease.

> *"One chance, that's all they give us...One Chance!"*
> - Will Smith in *Hitch*

Now, in your mind, you may be perfect for her: The One to make her happy, lift her up, fulfill all her dreams, and fill her with joy and peace the rest of her life. However, she will never know that unless and until you're genuine – AND she has a clear, open heart to notice you at all – and let you in to her space, and possibly, her life.

Get Yourself Ready For:
The First Look

Sometimes, you look into her eyes and it hits you: you just know you're getting together with that woman, for better or worse. This is never contrived or forced, and actually, has very little to do with who you are – or think you are. This is exactly how I met my last girlfriend.

73

Right then is when you look her in the eye and say the world's best pickup line:

"Hi."

That's it. That's what studies have shown is the best thing to say if you seek a true, emotional connection with a woman. And by the way, what's the best cologne you could use?

None.

Studies also show more women are attracted to men who smell like baby powder – as well as a man's natural scent – than anything else. Still, sometimes, the best thing to say is:

NOTHING. ZERO.

Let her speak first, however:

Be accessible.
Be courteous and respectful.
Blow off all the rules, words, regulations, and even this book when the time comes.

Being yourself is more than 95% of the men she meets are able to do...especially if she's good looking and has a dozen guys chasing her, which she probably does. Yes, ultimately, as stated, she is responsible for opening up to you, but after that, it's up to you to take charge.

Timing is everything. You can't go faster than her...nor slower, but you must go just slightly ahead...leading...and pulling...very gently.

74

If you catch her eye and you see a light, but then she won't look at you, don't take it personally...you just lost the moment, and it will never return with that woman.

The look is in the eyes, the windows to the soul; that's where genuine emotion...real connection starts...the connection with her heart – which runs her life, her decisions, her time and attention.

Without *The Look,* all else is futile; give up now; go get a beer. I think of Tom Hanks in *Forrest Gump: "Run Forrest, Run!"*

However, when you have The Look:

Talk less and stop jumping up and down like a raving moron...you will only sabotage yourself.

Be calm and confident
Be consistent
Demonstrate your self respect
Stand tall in the moment between her and you, and no one else
Be the rare guy who has something genuine to give; a place, a time, a rest from the cold, self-centered, anonymous dating scene.
A laugh, a smile, a warm, soft look.
Right at this moment:

Less is more.

Don't tell her you like or Love her (even if you do), until you're positive she already feels the same.

Again: What Do Women Want?

"A woman wants to be swept off her feet..."
- Kathleen Turner in the TV documentary: *The Science of Sex*

Sound simple?

Well, it is, and it isn't. Depends on who – and where you are right now, in your life. Kathleen was right then, and she's right now, but this only applies to men who still have a **strong, yet humble attitude** – (somewhat, but not totally impossible), and an immediate sense of romantic chemistry. **A man with more to Give than to Take.** Most of all: A man who's not all about sex.

Learn from your past.
Stand on the good of your past; but NEVER LIVE in your past.

The future is a dream
Tomorrow never comes
The past is not accessible
Be Present
Be here Now

Remember: TODAY, right now, is all you ever have.

PERFECT?

Despite what you've heard, a woman does not expect to find a "Perfect Man" because:

They know they don't exist.

<u>Become The Opposite of society's normal.</u>

After numerous trips to Europe, I got an idea of what too many "normal" American men look like to the rest of the world, and to many women as well: Loud-mouthed, overweight guys in bars or drunks who swear and babble on and on about sex and women, and yet again: go home alone. Ultimately, you must be more; rise above all this and be different. Work to slash your negatives to the bone – and see what remains.

Ever notice how much more cool, calm and quiet you are when you have a girlfriend/wife? Have you also noticed you seem to attract more women – when you have one already?

The next time you're unattached, imagine you're involved with the best woman you've ever met. Try to become that cool, calm (but now warmly outgoing and social), strong and genuine man you were back then, and see what happens.

Alright, here's another checklist; read it in front of a mirror:

A woman wants a man who is:

- ➤ Strong but not cocky
- ➤ Warm and Emotional, but not a Wimp or Pushover
- ➤ Humorous and Funny, but not Silly, Childish or Crude
- ➤ Genuinely Kind and Courteous to others as much as possible – she needs to see this in action, all the time
- ➤ Secure – not wrapped up in Drama with friends or family – and especially NOT talking about, or involved with - or talking to - an ex-girlfriend, wife, etc.
- ➤ Employed, but not all about Work or Money, which includes:

- ➤ Financially sound, but not Materialistic, Greedy or Cheap; besides, she is most likely working, and doing OK financially
- ➤ As clear as possible about his future plans regarding: Marriage and/or Children, Work, Where he'd like to live, and eventual retirement (don't even discuss these long-term items until your 3rd or 4th encounter, and only if pressed by her; then be honest)
- ➤ Clean and well-kept, but not anal or fastidious, either with clothing or housekeeping

> *"You're never as good, or as bad, as they say you are."*
> - George Clooney, during a brief TV interview

He should also:

- ➤ Listen more, talk less, and take a genuine interest in her life, what she does for fun, her friends and family
- ➤ Never rush the physical – which can only follow genuine Emotion and Chemistry (worth repeating)
- ➤ Keep outside interests: Volunteering, Hobbies, Church or Secular Community Groups, etc.
- ➤ Get a Life, dammit

Connect: Carefully

**The deeper you get into the life of another, the harder –
and more painful it is - to get out of their life.**

As hard as it is, as lonely as you might be: don't go down that
road unless you see something long-term happening – it will
only lead to another painful separation.

<u>Don't waste your time or hers.</u>

Trouble with boundaries? Then Henry Cloud's book
*Boundaries, When to Say YES, When to Say NO, and take
control of your life* is a must read. Be sure to check any of his
videos on You Tube, well worth it; he's the best.

Laugh it up, fuzzball

After the initial, in-the-eyes connection, lighten up. Tease, joke,
get silly, whatever you can do to make a woman smile, laugh
and forget herself.

Eventually, you'll learn about where she lives and works, but
this is not a job interview, nor a senate interrogation. Do not
bring up marriage, her ex-husband or last boyfriend, long-term
plans, etc. when you first meet. You can cover that down the
road. This is unofficial, this is off the imaginary "record," which
doesn't exist anyway. She's not a target or your next victim.
This is not a baseball game and you're not up to bat. This is
personal, like Lyle Lovett's *Private Conversation.*

Look around you; improvise; make creative observations and
connections; search for humor in people and places, it is
everywhere.

79

You could be babbling about camels in the streets of Tokyo and it wouldn't matter. It's not the content, it's the delivery. Remember Roger Daltrey and the WHO: *"It's the singer not the song, that makes the music move along."*

Find your music, and be it, 24/7.

Because for that brief moment you have together, every word or deed is just a metaphor. There's only one reason to get together again: to gaze again into warm eyes.

A woman needs to feel like you and her together are:

<u>Unique. Special. A one-of-a-kind couple.</u>

She needs to think she's the only woman on the planet you've ever been with – or will ever want to be with.

It's up to you to make her feel like that. NOT by bowing down and doing everything she wants, but as always: by keeping your dignity, connecting with your heart, and taking the lead.

Speak

Surveys show that up to 82% of women say they've been seduced by a man's voice. The sound of your voice, the tone and measure, the warmth...creates a pillow to rest her head.

Before you speak a single word:

She's watching how you talk, not hearing what you say, at least at the start. She's watching how you're saying it...body language, confidence, eye contact.

These are the things about you that create the "Love Attraction" promoted on Oprah years ago, (I heard someone call her "Umprah Humphrey" once) and *The Secret* movie. These are the intangibles that will either turn-on or turn-off every woman you meet, in that first moment.

Tell her: you just got out of prison – you're on work release. Aliens just dropped you off - back on the ship in 1 hour. Make her smile. The crazier, the better.

The Music Effect

Psychology has proven the profound effect of music on our moods, energy, focus and everyday lives. It greatly affects how we see ourselves and those around us; how we perceive our place in the world and with others; how we might be drawn to Love, or run from it.

What songs affected you the most growing up? Hard rock, pop rock, jazz, international? Here's a few songs that drove my independence and desire to run from committed relationships. Now that I'm more aware of influences like these, <u>I no longer run:</u>

Waiting on the World to Change, **John Mayer**
When Push Comes to Shove, **The Grateful Dead**
Misty Mountain Hop and *Your Time is Gonna Come,* **Led Zeppelin**
Ramblin' Man, **The Allman Brothers**
The Wanderer, **Dion**
Stone Free, **Jimi Hendrix**
Sweet Dreams (Are Made of This), **Eurythmics**

There are more songs like these, of course. Think back. Can you detach yourself from negative songs, or judgments made by others about why you didn't, or shouldn't commit now?

More often, of course, music brings people together. Take your woman to a concert, a bar, a street fest, anywhere to see her favorite tunes.

The God Illusion

When things are going great with a woman, avoid the trap of thinking you're God's gift to all women, that they all want you, that you're an amazing stud, or that they can't resist you.

<u>You're Not. They Don't. You're still Not. They Can.</u>

This is why when you find a good one – a good combination of you and her – don't change or think you can "upgrade" because:

You have arrived.

Stick with it. See where it goes.
The grass is NOT always greener.
Remember how much it sucks to "Date."

Timing: Love the One You're With

As mentioned, when you're already involved with a woman, other women are more attracted to you. That's because you're relaxed, confident, and content. Women sense this and are drawn to it. There's also women's unconscious, herd mindset: if they believe other women like or accept you, you're probably "OK."

Snap out of it.
You're still not God's gift to women:

This is Love's gift to you.

Respect it; don't abuse it, and don't get a big head. It's only good timing.

You're still the same Rat you always were,
just a happier, more contented Rat.

If you like the woman you're with, stay with her. Don't switch to another just because you can, or because you think you're some happening guy; it just seems that way because you're confident and pumped up from being with her. Try to play both ends, and you'll most likely end up with nothing.

Never try to prove yourself to yourself; YOU are the only one who sees your situation clearly – and God (or heart, spirit, etc.) of course – but no one else.

"You're the only one who sees - the changes you take yourself through..."
- Stevie Wonder

Don't Slam the Other Guy

Think back.

What was your first reaction when you believed your girlfriend or wife was attracted to someone else? Like most men, your knee-jerk reaction is to trash him; you talk him down; you try to talk her out of caring about him.

What then? The opposite happens: She wants him *more.*

That's because we're defiant creatures. It's in our nature to be drawn to that which seems forbidden, and being told to stay away from anything only makes us want it more. This can be especially true of women with weak or distant fathers, or who's ex-husband/boyfriend was too dominating, and now she's in that spiteful, backlash mode – even if it's a subconscious reaction.

Instead, stand on your own terms. Be strong in your own, personal value. If she's wise enough to see it, no one will be able to distract her from you.

In fact, if possible, confront the guy, right in front of her. Shake his hand and introduce yourself. Make a good impression. show you're mature and not intimidated. Be sincere. That's impressive and proves you're secure within yourself. That's how you'll keep her – or at least show you're not jealous.

Men Need Brothers

Build allies wherever you can in this life: Men need other men to process and channel their thoughts, their energy, their fears, emotions and desires. This is not childish, weak, gay or 'sensitive', this is essential to the sanity of our world, and that includes your world.

Talk to good friends or family you trust and have the guts to be vulnerable. Speak and process everything on your mind, heart, and soul. If they laugh at you, give them this book and move on – they need it more than you.

I enjoy building and fixing things. I want to see how things work so I can fully understand them, repair them and know what I'm talking about. In high school, I took classes in automotive repair, metals and woods fabrication, electronics and so on. I would build models, or tear things apart and put them back together. I've worked in home construction, on farms and in white-collar jobs at major corporations. I eventually started my own company and wrote 10 published books. I've traveled and explored art, history and culture in 30 countries and counting.

Here's my point: I could not have done any of this without the support of good friends and family.

By now you've traveled, researched technologies, investments, cars and politics. You're smart, have worked hard and reaped the rewards. Now: what should we as men do with the time, effort and knowledge we've applied to ourselves – our hearts and minds?

We get what we give

It is long past time for men to gain greater fulfillment with ourselves, our lives, our communities, and with the women we meet. We get the best out of others when we give our best to them – because in the end if we don't, we end up alone, and you know what?

<u>That just really sucks.</u>

Women Need Sisters

I've met too many women living afraid and isolated. They have been burned in possessive relationships; they're afraid to open up to men. But the women I know who bond with other women are consistently more positive, upbeat, mentally and physically healthier, and just better off. They also have a better chance of meeting a decent man.

Deep social connections have been shown to increase longevity, strengthen the immune system, and support cognitive functions. But they take time – and attention – to sustain.

- Experience Life Magazine, November, 2017

PART FIVE

Love Is:

Mutual Hypnosis

(and nice teeth).

But it is also:

Humble
Warm
Kind
Patient
About the other person

Your standards

Your standards, your pride and ego will always tell you you're doing great, fine, wonderful, and that all your decisions are right, accurate, truthful and honorable...

Look back at those big decisions - the ones about which women to get involved with, sleep with, commit to, etc., and ask yourself:

1. What were the results?
2. How did it end up?
3. Are you really where you want to be?

"God is in charge," a gal-pal said the other day.

God, fate, or however you define it, may have you sitting across from someone who would be excellent for you. However, only you can choose to open or close yourself, your heart, to that person – or not.

I have a good, smart friend who puts women on pedestals. He emulates them too much, and wherever we go, he asks questions about their personal life and always seeks their approval. It could be a waitress, someone he just met, it doesn't matter. This gets very annoying. He's married now, but at the time, this smacked of insecurity: Why the need for constant attention and acknowledgement from total strangers, male or female? Do you always need to be the center of attention?

The woman is not always right just because she's sexy – don't agree with anyone based on their looks.

Takers & Givers

We've become a nation of takers, not givers, and that's no good for anyone. As long as you're forever in 'take' mode, with that 'me first' attitude, you will never be content in this life. You'll be reading self-help books like this forever, until the day you die, alone...with dirty dishes and laundry piled up. Your family and friends will need to hire someone to clean your place and sell all your junk.

Now: Is that a pretty sight? No.

IT SUCKS!

Over? Don't Block Yourself

Nothing's over until it can no longer be retrieved, rescued, brought back to life.

It's not over until it seems totally pointless to talk to her. Until then, you're essentially blocking each other from finding someone else.

Until then, a failing encounter is like a fish stuck on the beach, flopping and gasping for air. The water either surges to bring it back from the cold dry land, or it doesn't.

> *"A relationship, I think, is like a shark, it has to constantly move forward, or it dies. I think what we've got on our hands, is a dead shark."*
> - Woody Allen, *Annie Hall*

You can be patient, kind, open-hearted, and try to push the fish back into the water, and it still may not matter.

Once you break a woman's heart, or she breaks yours, you can change, and learn, and grow from it.

But you can't go back to <u>her,</u> and:

You Can't Be Friends

<u>If/when it finally comes to it:</u>

Always make a clean break – don't drag it out.
It's cold, it's nasty, it sucks. It's also the best way out for you
and her, <u>no matter whose idea it is to end it.</u>

There are No Good Breakups

Remember: All "relationships" with the opposite sex can end in
only one of four ways:

1. A painful breakup, where you never talk again
2. Marriage, followed eventually by divorce. The (default?)
choice of around 50% of all married couples in America. You
never - or rarely, see or talk to each other, unless of course you
have kids
3. You remain "friends" but rarely see or talk to each other – for
whatever that's worth
4. Marriage that lasts "'til death do us part." If my parents can
do this, so can you

*As long as you're both still talking about anything, or trying to
be "nice," neither of you are free to move on.*

Cut Your Losses

Whatever you do: don't be a PEST. Know when to walk away, and that's usually sooner rather than later. Nothing's worse than a yelping Chihuahua that grabs on to your pant leg and won't let go.

Cut your words down:

Remember that even the end of a connection, if it must end, is about feeling free and released.

Get Out

Get out and meet real women, right now. In the grocery store, or at business networking and sporting events. Volunteer; take an improv acting class; get involved in your community, and go to every party and gathering you can.

Life is boring and pointless without a woman. Men (and yes women too) are not meant to be alone. We need more than sex. We're meant to be in love, and here's the best description of that:

> *"Love is patient and is kind; love does not envy. Love does not brag, is not proud, doesn't behave itself inappropriately, does not seek its own way, is not provoked, takes no account of evil; doesn't rejoice in unrighteousness, but rejoices with the truth; bears all things, believes all things, hopes all things, endures all things.*
> *Love never fails."*
> - 1 Corinthians 13:4-8
> New Heart English Bible, (NHEB: JE)

Or perhaps Love is this:

Two people deciding (or pretending) not to notice the messed up, sinful past and obvious flaws of the other, and instead focusing on the positive: their smiles, their tone of voice, their eyes, their good deeds and intentions – as best as they can see them.

So what are you doing?
Are you kidding me?

Put this down, right now, because E.B. White once said:

HUMOR can be dissected as a frog can, but the thing dies in the process, and the innards are discouraging to any but the pure scientific mind.

The same is certainly true of Love.

Turn off your computer and i-Pad. Drop your cell phone, because all that texting and emailing, all the Match.coms and eHarmonys and all that online crap means absolutely NOTHING if you get out and talk, communicate and connect with a living-breathing female.

Motivation and Reminders

APPENDIX – I

Easy

It all used to be so easy.
You meet a woman, you hit it off. Done.
Good times, laughs, trips to sunny beaches.

What happened?

We grew up
We got hurt
We got scared
We got selfish
We got picky
We're anxious

Now it's all about ourselves: having everything we want, how we want it, when we want it. **We are spoiled brats.**

Every man wants the perfect composite woman, and actually expects her to be single...alone...ready, willing and able...and actually spending money on Match.com, looking "just for you..."

Are you looking for Ms. Right, or Ms. Right Now? Do you actually expect to find the gorgeous woman with just the right face, right height, and small hips. THE ONE who is:

Not sleazy, but not boring?
Smart, but not selfish or mean?
Warm and affectionate, but not needy?
Kind, giving, generous and loving, but not a pushover?

Guess what: most of them are at home with their husbands and kids. But you don't have to end up a lonely old man wandering a beach in Florida with a metal detector.

It works both ways. As one female stand-up comedian put it: *"I'm no longer looking for Mr. 'Right', I'm looking for Mr.' You'll Do.'"*

There are always a few good ones left; their last encounter is over, or they've been too chicken to get married.

Hey, to quote Sting: *you're not alone in being alone.* There's 20,000 singles a day signing up on Match.com, but that includes men and women; that's according to, of course, Match.com. Truth is, many of them are still married, attached, or just messed up.

Choices

Perhaps you're single by choice:

You seek perfection
You like peace and quiet
You like your privacy
You want a Playboy model

What are you, a Hermit?

The Untouchable Woman

The world is filled with "tough" macho guys, trapped in a world of fear by their own lust, the very lust that keeps them cold and alone. They're living in the same impossible fantasy splattered on TV and cell phone screens, magazine covers and billboards all over the country.

They don't know what to say, how to be natural, caring and warm, how not to look like just another jerk trying to hit on another beautiful woman for sex; holding back the same tired lines she's heard a thousand times. I've seen a few guys give it a try, but nothing seems to stick; they go home alone.

They are disconnected from:

- Their Hearts and Emotions
- A Higher Power/Cause/Purpose
- Unselfish love

Just like them, until you place a high priority on all of those things, you will remain alone - as it should be.

Remember the Bob Seger song: *Beautiful Loser, You Just Can't Have It All.* Seger was right. But what he really meant was: you can't have everything, or every woman you see, and you certainly don't need more than one.

When you think of Seger's *all* as something different, when you see it as fulfillment, about quality over quantity, about a true partnership...
About genuine connection and communication about everyday things...

About much more than great sex, no matter how great it may be:

Then maybe you CAN have it all - or get pretty damn close, with ONE decent woman.

Sacrificial Love between the two of you will be all you need. As long as it's real, as long as you believe, as long as it's genuine, it can last a lifetime. It can happen – believe it. You must have faith, or it will never happen.

"Nuts" is a pretty broad term

If you have been even slightly emotionally involved with a woman, or fallen madly in bed a few times, then here's the deal:

It could be you've already met THE ONE, you just didn't know it at the time. You felt good and comfortable around her; she just didn't meet your impossibly high expectations, your parameters, your "standards."

You just weren't ready for the c-word: Commitment. You told yourself you weren't ready. You wanted to travel, make more money, meet other women and "play the field." Talk about a weak, cheesy rationale for men who fear commitment!

Don't get me wrong. Not every woman you've met, kissed or been physical with wanted the C-word; maybe they just wanted company. Maybe in the big picture, you were just using each other. Sounds crude, but it happens all the time.

Alright, so now that's done with, and both of you missed out. It was exciting, it felt good, your ego got even bigger, along with other body parts. But where did it go? Do you remember the pain when it was over? Where is she now? More importantly:

Where is your chemistry, your spark, your emotion, your attraction? Call it what you will; it is beyond words, timeless and nameless.

I Did it My Way

I never felt the need to get married in my 20s or 30s. I'd tell my friends about my most recent attachment and they'd say: "Why ruin it by getting married?" More bad advice from good friends. Interesting how it's seems OK to have been married and gone through a terrible divorce, than to have never been married and avoided divorce all together.

 Back then the popular quotes were:
"Why buy the loaf, when you can get it by the slice?"
"Why buy the cow, when you can get the milk for free?"

For me now, later in life, marriage is a great idea - at last.

It Happens All the Time

Check out any mall or sporting event; you see the most bizarre couples and combinations. Beautiful women with sloppy guys devoid of table manners. Every other word is four letters, and not the good kind; sometimes half-drunk, sometimes fully drunk. Good, smart, great looking women will even marry (then often divorce) these guys.

A man will also cut a woman plenty of slack to be with her. In our looks-oriented society, he will do what he must to be with the most beautiful woman that puts up with his lame jokes and ugly tie, even if they're totally incompatible, and that is a big mistake. How long can it last? Where's the dignity?

The Urgency of Now

Most of the time, when you meet a new person - male or female - you quickly become a part of their life, or you don't. Whether you know it or not, you've done this to both men and women all around you, all your life. Women know there's no in-between when it comes to chemistry and romance.

Unless you really are connected to your heart, your emotions, and really have warmth, security and love to give, then logic, sex and the media are your driving factors - the latest techniques and motivation for the hunt. You see the rabbit, grab your spear, and the chase begins.

With women, in business, and in mixed social circles, it's just the opposite. People need depth, honesty, sincerity, romance and emotion, and they need to see it right now.

Always In The Moment, and Confident

When you're the first one to lighten up, to tease - and seize - the moment, you prove you are confident, like Kelsey Grammer on Frasier: *"There's no aphrodisiac like confidence..."* You must remain:

- Here, now, in the present moment.
- Focused on HER, which, let's face it, is what's most important to her.
- Not intimidated by her looks; nor apparently, anything else. For that moment, and for all she knows, YOU are the definition of *backbone*.

Write your own story in the moment. NEVER prepare or practice your lines. Study Lao Tzu's *Tao Te Ching.* There are no lines, no perfect words or techniques. If you happen to be having a bad day when you meet the best woman on the planet, then that's just too bad. Unfair? You bet it is.

There is only the moment – grab it asap. Then, as in the John Cusack film: *Say Anything,* put your heart and soul on the line, you will survive no matter what happens. Women will notice; if not right away, then eventually. Never give up.

I hereby offer you refuge; a place of rest; solace and above all Peace. If you get nothing else from this book, remember these things:

Don't try so hard to connect

Yes, you can and should tune-in to who she is, but don't drive yourself crazy. It's not worth it, it doesn't work, it's awkward, and only pushes people away. It could be you're only meant to be friends. I have quite a few gal-pals I hang out with, dance/go to movies with, and catch up with at parties.

Don't do anything like anyone else

This is a great mantra for a lousy day, try it. (Send me an email...let me know if it works....)

Get Out of Your Way

Be yourself, yes, but first get your fear and insecurity out of the way to let personal, private, <u>mutual chemistry</u> happen – or not – in the moment. Show up as much as possible, and see what hits you.

Ask any woman what they want in a man, and they'll recite the same tired lines: "Someone who's stable and kind and strong; a man who's honest and reliable; someone I can look up to; someone who's just a normal, *nice* guy with a good heart."

Horse Crap. How many women actually wait for a man like this?

With few exceptions (and we all like to think we're the exception, myself included), most women will also tell you that type of man is either already married or gay. Besides, some men are alone and available because maybe they have great, unselfish hearts and plenty of attention and kindness to give, but they're not good at that first moment...the first 30 seconds they meet a woman...and so they give a wrong first impression, and go home alone.

Unfair? Yes it is, but it's also unfair to most women. Because as we've seen, most women are either 'taken' by a man at first impression, or left cold.

More women need to be aware of this, and give us a break. Too often, they're attracted to players, guys who know how to say and do all the right things to attract/seduce a woman in the first 30 seconds, yet have no heart, soul, kindness or commitment left in them. These men are all on the same path to nowhere.

However much planning and strategizing you may use to get close to - and connect - with a woman, most of the time it will not work. Ask yourself; does she need a man in her life right now – or does she seem totally self contained? Because sometimes:

> *"A woman needs a man like a fish needs a bicycle..."*
> *- Irina Dunn*

Tease her, tickle her brain. You gotta be fun: her personal entertainment director. That's more than going out on the town, it's being spontaneous, unique, and above all, exciting, warm and romantic at the right time. Point out the strange and unique. Take her to a different place; not just an exotic vacation, but a different place inside. This is not manipulation; it's having fun with a woman, showing your creative side, and lifting her up. Grab a kiss goodnight if you can, on the first or second meeting. Fail to do this, and she may assume you're weak, not interested, can't take the lead, etc.

This is how you become the vacation, the private place to go, the one she can trust; the one to have fun with and just call spontaneously. Now that's Chemistry, and it's not to be taken lightly. Without that, what's the point of all those logic-stuffed subjects that make us yawn and drag us down? We NEED to break the monotony, the boredom and loneliness of ourselves.

Examples

The best movies take us to wild places; they show us people with daring and talent...filled with life and love, possibility and power. They're doing the risky, daring things most of us only dream about. That's what you need to be, to attract a woman worth the rest of your time, attention, and life.

Maybe the closest most of us will get to movie stardom is travel. Take long & short vacations whenever you can; escape your job and everyday monotony. You're Luke Skywalker, destroying your demons; you're Indiana Jones, fighting for righteousness.

The Eyes are Still the Windows to the Soul

I'll never forget one night in a dance club. Most of us were up and around, talking and catching up with our friends. Some men were trying to talk-up women at the bar. Then I noticed two guys just sitting on a sofa in the middle of the room. They just sat there and made eye contact with every woman that walked by...or they didn't.

That's how they met women; they could read their eyes. If the woman looked into their eyes for just a few extra seconds, these guys would eventually walk over and start talking, always keeping eye contact...always showing up...being there for her, in the critical, first few minutes.

105

Many times, from the women I've talked to, and that's quite a few before writing this, this leads to one of the old lines we've all heard:
"It just happened"
"We just knew it"
"It was Instant Chemistry"

Love is Blind?

Love is not blind, it is we who are blind to love.

If humans were in charge of Love, we would only destroy it. We wreck most important things in this life: Peace, Harmony, Justice, the Environment, and a really decent pair of shoes. If men were truly in control of falling in love, then we'd all be living happily ever after with the woman of our dreams.

Handle the wacky times

We've all been there: A woman gives you her phone number; you call and maybe get together a few times; maybe there's not that intense Chemistry from the beginning, but you're willing to give it a shot. Then after a few days, she sets a time to get together, maybe stop by your house and have dinner. But then, surprise: something came up, last minute, she's so sorry, and promises to make it up to you "next week." What do you do? Stand firm and say, "Hey, no problem, I understand...some other time?"

Well, this understanding, "Nice Guy" approach may work some of the time, especially at the start. But in the long run, does this really work?

She Doesn't Want to See You

Of course no one can make every appointment, but if she really wanted to see you – to get involved in your life at any level – she would make the time, or quickly set another time to meet.

It can all get very frustrating. People misunderstand, make wrong assumptions about you and walk away. What do you do? Get angry? Are you kidding?

Your Anger Doesn't Matter

Imagine you're in a conversation - any conversation - with a woman, a man, a business associate, your 12-year-old son. Things start to heat up; they're getting under your skin and you're both acting like idiots.

It's ego vs. ego. You start to get angry, and you start to show it. Your anger is totally justifiable in your mind, and given time, the other person may very well agree that your anger is righteous. But here's the catch:

Once you become angry, the focus of the entire conversation has now become: YOUR ANGER. Now the other person is off the hook. They're no longer thinking about the dumb, inconsiderate thing they did to provoke your justifiable anger. Instead, they're focused on you and the spectacle you're making of yourself. You've lost the argument already.

More important: All the talk and anger will not change them one bit, nor their future behavior toward you, and could actually push them away.

In reality, *you* haven't "lost" anything, although your pride and ego may be hurt (awww...) and your frustration is totally justified. The truth is you've both lost, because you've missed a chance to change and grow closer with that person. Ultimately of course, life and relationships aren't about winning arguments.

More Unspeakables

A gal-pal of mine once said she was having a "DTR" talk with her most recent encounter. To her, that stood for: "Define the Relationship." OK: I'll just contact my attorney and we'll draw up a contract. Barf. To me, DTR stands for: "Destroy the Relationship."

How well you can sustain a connection of any kind, be it sexual, friendly, romantic or true love (as in humble commitment and unselfish sacrifice to another) will ultimately depend on your faith and belief that Love is possible at all.

You've heard it over and over: "You must lose yourself to find yourself." We hear it in Christianity, in Taoism, in just about all the major religions. So what does it mean? It means:

You are not the center of the universe. God (i.e., true, unselfish Love) IS at the center of everything – our only reason to be: to work, to play, to speak, to show up anywhere.

The Bible's pretty clear on this: "Love thy neighbor as thyself..." But it also says: "Love God (Love) before all else, even yourself or your neighbor. I admit, that's a tough one for me; where does "I" end and God begin? Remember: The experience of Love or excitement, romance, pleasure, etc., is a gift from God (Love).

Do not abuse it, and make it merely a means to physical pleasure. With the worldwide economy, especially the US, running on sex, sex, and more sex, this is what the vast majority of humankind does every day.

"It's in the way that you use it...boy don't you know. And if you lie you will lose it, feelings will show...so don't you ever abuse it, don't let it go..."

- Eric Clapton

I challenge you to look deeper and reach higher – to be more and find a better standard than yourself. I am not religious, but Jesus is the best standard I've found. Christianity was never meant to be a "religion" filled with rules and guilt. Ultimately, it's a mind shift, a faith in something better and more stable than you, a *release* from guilt, pain, arrogance and personal suffering. For too many men, this is hard to grasp: we think we must carry the world, and the weight of or selfishness on our shoulders or we're not "real" men.

Of course you will never be Jesus, and no one expects you to be. You will always fall short – that's a given.

But you've got to start somewhere; why not here and now, and every day moving forward? No one on earth can truly know or comprehend everything about you. Ultimately, only you and God can understand you: who you are, what you've been through, how you spend your time, or why you sacrifice your time and effort for others. God sees your ultimate intention in everything you do, and ultimately, so do you, if you're not afraid to look.

PANCREAS - II

Alone Yet?

Before you head out there, *remember PART TWO above:*

Are you <u>alone</u> yet? Because a real, true, Single Man must be:

In a lonely place, but still:

Strong in conviction
Unsettled, yet calm and focused
Confident, but not cocky
Always thinking, always observing
Lean, Sparse, Ready
In a state of creative tension
Daring - a risk taker
Clear
Uncomfortable, but always in:

The Moment

And always on some creative:

Edge

Because if you really think you're "complete" without a woman, then my friend, you are lying to yourself.

If you really want to be *In Love* with a woman, then find the true love in, and for, yourself – and show it. Because until you've done that, you will certainly NOT connect in true Love with a real woman.

More reasons not to bring up the past

When the first impression you give is that you've had lousy encounters in the past, women will - if subconsciously - see you as defective, even if you were deceived by unstable women, even if you're the greatest guy in the world...they will project their future with you based on the past you tell them about. This is your past with their fellow women, *with whom they bond subconsciously.*

They'll typically side with, and believe, 'the other woman,' even one they've never met, before a man.

The women you meet also have a past, but just like you, they want a new start. Turn it all around and speak the positive. This is the only way to create a new, stable future with women you meet. The past is gone, and if you need a few months on your own, away from meeting new women, then do it: learn guitar, play racquetball or golf. Get counseling. Re-watch *Jason Bourne.*

Rebuild

I discussed rebuilding yourself after a break up. Rebounding from one heartbreak to the next is no way to go through life. To do anything else is unfair to you, your future and the women you've not yet met.

I've mentioned this to many women and they seem surprised and impressed. They think it's a great idea, and say most men they meet don't do this - they're always on the prowl for the next victory or conquest - and that never works.

When all the crap is stripped away, what are you left with?

A LACK of immaturity, selfishness, lust, cheesy pickup lines and disrespectful behavior...a lack of negatives. When both men and women just stop trying to be George Clooney or Megan Fox, they become far more attractive, interesting, accessible, sincere and likeable.

You had this person in you all the time, it's just hidden behind all the junk and fear; all the neediness and lack of patience that drives off the genuine eye contact (The Look), the connection women need, just to keep on talking to your ugly mug.

Do You Deserve Greatness?

Are you there yet? Are you the writer of your life? Or is God, or some sort of better, higher power? Are you in the tension, on the edge, learning, creating and growing?

Because you know of course:

We all come into this world **Alone,** and we all leave it **Alone.** What happens in between, what you make of yourself, your reality, your situation, is entirely up to you, and absolutely no one else. Not your mother or father, your boss or your ex. No one else but YOU. No one else can take the blame, nor the credit, for what you are, and what you can become. Could it be otherwise?

Care

The opposite of Love isn't hate, it's apathy – not caring – not giving a damn – and walking back into: the anonymous crowd.

If you've ever missed a woman's attention, it is only because you blinked; you looked away, you hesitated. You didn't say hello after you caught eyes and she walked near.

I did this years ago at my health club. My eyes caught those of the most beautiful woman in the building. She was always running or on the weight machines. Always alone. Even the gym rats didn't have the nerve to walk up and just talk to her.

Then one day, our eyes collided.

She looked right at me, and I looked back – she walked over...right up to me...looking into my eyes...and I looked into hers; all I had to do was say one single word:

Hi.

But I didn't.

She walked by, and said nothing. She couldn't have said anything – it was not her place to speak.

That moment, when we could have met, for better or worse, was over. Now when I see her, she looks away...as she must.

That fate-given (God-given?) moment is gone...forever, and can never return... Seize those moments – whenever you can.

Trust

Be careful whom you trust. I'll never forget the complete and total betrayal by one of my best gal-pals because I didn't want to get physical with her. I trusted her, even loved her like a sister, and over several years, she would cry on the phone about how much she wanted a man in her life.

On two separate occasions, she said to my face: "I want to see you naked..." I swear I can't make this stuff up. I told her over and over how great she was, and in so many words, that I just wasn't physically attracted. She was a fun, smart woman, and I told her she'd find someone. At last, after years of loneliness, she met a great guy, and I was happy for her.

To my amazement, and out of pure spitefulness, she took ideas I had shared about running my business and began to compete directly against me – after promising for four years she would never do such a thing. She then proceeded to lie about me to mutual friends. Nice, huh? Talk about 'hell hath no fury…'

Trusting the wrong person, in work, love, whatever, can cost you:

Your time
Your job
Your income
Your friendships
Your heart…until you rebuild it.

Work less often; you will die with money in the bank; it just doesn't matter. Though you should not speak it, only the "R" word matters: Relationships.

Be present; in the here and now, as much as you can.

THIS IS NOT A DRESS REHEARSAL

Forget the day: Seize every moment to build, create and renew yourself. Now is all you ever have. If you settle for less, THAT is what you get.

Get Off the Sidelines

Are you on the sidelines of your own life - a victim of JD Salinger's "Death of Imagination?" Do you really think you're in "control" of your life? Because I ask you: How's that workin' out? Why do you need to answer all of this - even if you don't want to?

Because at this point in your life, time is not just passing, it's speeding up - faster than ever. It's warp speed and Captain Kirk is off the bridge. The stars, the planets, the galaxies are flying by, but who's at the helm, you? God? A higher purpose? Exactly where are you heading? You know it: time waits for no one – so ACT on it, right now. Less is more; be different, be a mystery, project a future.

Stand in Defiance

Stand against boring, predictable social expectations. Sometimes, giving someone exactly what they want and expect, is the last thing they need.

This defines your:
Backbone
Dignity
Stature
Boundaries

And most important, this gives her a strong image to:
Respect
Follow
Admire
Latch on to and:
Gives her a place to rest her head and invest her emotions.

Stand your ground and speak up. In the media and the workplace, mature men are too often taken for granted, sidelined, considered bland and predictable even before they speak, and too many allow themselves to accept - and fall into this image.

Get out of the house and EXERCISE, Damn It

You're eating too much fast food - you have brain fog, the fat and gluten is clogging your brain, your blood sugar's out of whack; you're hyperglycemic. Don't become an "Average American": Out of shape, in debt, out of motivation, in the doldrums, alone behind a computer, a tablet, a cell phone. In trouble.

Be glad about one thing: You got this book, and it's time you get this straight, Meat Sack:

To the American Woman, You and I, my friend, are fully, quickly and completely: Replaceable. We've become a pair of shoes, a handbag, a car. When you understand this, you'll know you are not truly alone – you share this with all men.

"Strength and honor..."
- Russell Crowe in *Gladiator*

Be the Gladiator, every day. Stand by any noble values you have, demonstrate them, and live them every day, with everyone you meet, even when it feels like no one cares. People see you and notice, at the store, at work, at church, at the hockey game, at the health club. We hear the word "judge" all the time: "Don't judge me... this... that..." What we really mean is: *condemn*.

120

But all of us judge each other every second of every day. We are judged as much by what we speak, as by what we hold back.

Forgive – live in gratitude.
Serve others – it will all come back to you.

It's the women, as 'nuts' as they may seem, who often reveal the truth about ourselves – we learn it from the good women.

LIVER - III

Faith, and Things to Remember

Believe it's possible first – you must have faith: belief in things yet unseen. I've been in great situations...maybe you have too...but it didn't last, for the reasons already mentioned.

Now it's time to believe that it can last, forever.

Remember:

If you've ever had that buzz, that mutual love with a woman, it's not because you're great – you're not – you were just lucky. You were in the right place at the right time. It was God (the scraps of Love we're all born with) that did it, not you. In fact, you got there with that woman because *YOU* were out of the way...

　　　...unconscious...vulnerable...seducible by:

God/Love/Connection/Chemistry/Genuine, unselfish: Emotion

Experiencing these things is all that makes life worth living, surviving, enduring, tolerating, in this nasty world of insensitive, selfish people who walk and talk on this thin crust of earth.

Sex without love of course, is Pointless. Even damaging to your life, your body, your soul. So, why do it? Because society, or your friends, think you should?

You choose your future every single day - whether you know it or not - in all the little choices you make:

Which woman to call...
to look at...

to spend time with...
to cook salmon and pasta for...
to kiss.

You = Not Perfect

We hear the "P" word all the time now. You, of course, will never be perfect; there's no reason to be, so stop trying. Create a tension and keep the mystery...of you and where it's going... keep it in the moment... and make the moments count... Only you can build a cage around you – and only you have the key. I know it might sound stupid, dumb, silly, sappy, but that key is:

Sincerity

STOP MAKING SENSE – AGAIN

As men we find this counter-intuitive, but remember that Love, romance and commitment begin with feeling good... getting a thrill from another person...excitement, passion, desire, someone to hang out with. Keep it spontaneous.

GIRLS – and Women – just wanna have fun

Never be nervous; aim for fun/funny...even wacky. Just be easier to be with than most of the dweebs she meets...because like it or not, that's who she's comparing you to, right from the start.

Come across as a pushover and she'll immediately lose the number one emotion she must have for you: respect.

The glass will never be "full" with anyone; it's either ½ full or ½ empty. If not a drop, move on. Remember that perfection does not exist...certainly not in you or me. Why seek it in her?

Sexual tension - the chemistry that just seems to happen between men and women attracted to each other – is often traced back to pheromones. Does it matter? Sometimes, it just happens...you just click, or you don't. We take aspirin and prescription pills to relieve tension in our lives, but life is all about tension.

Always read between the lines because:

Words are boring. Words don't really matter. Everything's a metaphor that points to your:

Attitude
State of Mind
Core Values
Heart – or lack of it

And that, my friend, is how you will be judged as a:

Viable Boyfriend
Lover
Husband

Because people hear your tone. Cultivate a warm circle of community around you, even if you get stabbed in the back – remember that stabbing back only makes you just like them. Rise above it all.

Stay cool. Stay calm; she will relax with you

And that's it. You're home free. You have her heart, that is all you need.

Take time off to relax, kick back, get centered. Realize you can't have it all, or do it all, ever.

Most of all: Remember all you really need is One Woman, to give to, not take from. No more than that.

Now it's time to stop analyzing. Throw this book out.
Be yourself.
No one else can do it for you.

The hardest thing a real man can do? Rise above his body. Even former presidents, like Bill Clinton, a Rhode's scholar and sharp decision maker, couldn't do this, and it changed the results of the Bush/Gore election.

Be more. Control your sex drive, and you're on the path to a much higher, daily satisfaction with the opposite sex: A place to rest your heart, your joy, your problems, not just your body parts.

If you need help to do the above, find it. Get the counseling you need; open up to good friends who communicate at your level.

I've met so many people who spend their lives trying to fit better within a box they don't know they've created; but it's a box they can and must do without to grow and reach their highest potential. Everyone can do this; it only takes genuine, constant, persistent effort – looking at your situation and saying: "Enough is enough; I want outta here."

Find your box, and break out of it.
Find your chains, and smash them.

- ➢ Risk it all, but don't over-analyze and destroy the chemistry
- ➢ You can only be involved with one at a time; there's no such thing as two girlfriends/partners. If you think you have two girlfriends, you have nothing
- ➢ Looks don't matter so much
- ➢ GOD is Love and Love is personal – it is everywhere when you clear your heart and mind. Maybe that's all you need to know

Now get out there, and connect with a decent woman.

Greatness awaits.

Notes to Yourself

Whom or what do you need to clear/remove from your life that is keeping you from moving forward and connecting with a new woman? Friends? Ex-wives? Girlfriends? Make a list:

_____

_____

_____

_____

_____

_____

_____

_____

_____

_____

_____

What steps can you begin to take, today, to begin clearing out old emotions and former connections that are holding you back?

_____

_____

_____

_____

_____

_____

_____

_____

_____

_____

_____

How did you benefit from this book?

_____

_____

_____

_____

_____

_____

_____

_____

_____

_____

How will you change to compensate and improve in areas mentioned in this book: aligning with God/Love in your daily life?

_____

_____

_____

_____

_____

_____

_____

_____

_____

_____

_____

How will you change to compensate and improve in areas not mentioned in this book?

_____

_____

_____

_____

_____

_____

_____

_____

_____

_____

Rock Stars Arrested After Historic Flight

The Average White Band met up with Black Sabbath one Seventh Dream Day. They decided to take a cosmic trip in a Led Zeppelin flown by Twenty-One Pilots and Jimi Hendrix, who told everyone he was Grateful Dead.

After a near collision with Commander Cody and his Lost Planet Airmen, not to mention a highjack attempt by a Gang of Four, they closed the Doors and the Starship lifted higher and higher, over 10,000 Maniacs and Talking Heads, all Residents in a very Crowded House.

But Captain Beyond, Mr. Hendrix, was flying at speeds INXS of 801 Miles Davis per hour, when the Plastic Ono Steeler's Wheel broke off in his Badfingers. They called Dr. Dre, who rapped a bandage, but could not find a Cure. To make matters worse, the Weather Report was not good that day. The Aztec Camera was showing a Deep Purple sky over a Pink Floyd Mountain in Oregon.

He told them all to turn down the Roxy Music and hold on to their Heart, it would take no Little Feat to get out of this Big Mess, and they could soon be Slammin' Watusis.

But everyone stayed Cool and The Gang landed in a grove of Chuck Berry trees with a Clash.

The Police showed up and Men Without Hats locked everyone up.

Ozzie Osborne bit into a Fleetwood Mac and said they should have taken the Velvet Underground instead.

Made in the USA
Lexington, KY
08 March 2018